# THE SHIFT

## SCALE YOUR BUSINESS AND MULTIPLY YOUR WEALTH WITHOUT SACRIFICING YOU

## KIM WALSH PHILLIPS

broad
book
press

Broad Book Press, Publisher
Cover and interior design by Andrew Welyczko, AbandonedWest Creative, Inc.

Paperback ISBN: 978-1-73751-780-1
eBook ISBN: 978-1-73751-781-8

Published in the United States by Broad Book Press, an imprint of Broad Book Group, Edwardsville, IL.

Library of Congress Control Number: 2022920722

# CONTENTS

**BEFORE YOU READ THIS BOOK** ...................... v

**01: POWER GOALS** ........................................ 1
Having an Empire Business and Lifestyle Business
at the Same Time

**02: POWER WHYS** ......................................... 7
And How They Create Your Bottom Line

**03: POWERFUL PLANNING** ............................. 15
The Five North Stars to Success (aka The Thing You Want
to Skip Over But Is Here On Purpose, So Read It Anyway)

**04: POWERFULLY SIMPLE** .............................. 27
The Apex Accelerator (How to Easily Fill Your Business
with Clients You Love Working With)

**05: POWERFUL PROSPECTING** ......................... 37
Your Apex Alex and Ally... Giving All Your Attention to
Your Right-Fit Client

**06: POWERFUL LEAD GENERATION** ................... 47
Creating an Endless Supply of Quality Leads

**07: A POWERFUL PROFESSIONAL** ..................... 85
Power Thinking vs. Common Thinking

**08:** **STANDING OUT IN A SEA OF SAMENESS** . . . . . . . . 93
How to Create Your Own Unfair Competitive Advantage

**09:** **POWERFUL PROFITS** . . . . . . . . . . . . . . . . . . . . . . . . . . . . 101
Turning Your Prospects into Sales on Autopilot
with the Winning Webinar Blueprint

**10:** **THE POWERFUL PRESENTATION** . . . . . . . . . . . . . . . . . 107
The Winning Webinar

**11:** **THE POWERFUL PROFITABLE
BUSINESS SECRET** . . . . . . . . . . . . . . . . . . . . . . . . . . . . . 145
A Course

**12:** **THE POWERFUL SALES MACHINE** . . . . . . . . . . . . . . . . 151
From Course to Next Sale

**13:** **MAKING YOUR HIGH-TICKET OFFER** . . . . . . . . . . . . 173
By Scott Whitaker

**14:** **POWERFULLY POURING FUEL
ON THE FIRE** . . . . . . . . . . . . . . . . . . . . . . . . . . . . . . . . . . 187
Powering On Your Impact and Income Multiplier

**IN CONCLUSION** . . . . . . . . . . . . . . . . . . . . . . . . . . . . . . 191
You Can, And You Will

**THE POWERFUL PROFESSIONALS MOTTO** . . . . . . 193

**ACKNOWLEDGMENTS** . . . . . . . . . . . . . . . . . . . . . . . . . . . 195

# BEFORE YOU READ THIS BOOK

## The Definition of a Powerful Professional

**PUT DOWN THE** cocktail/mocktail/remote/golf club and pay attention to something important you need to know.

If you want to get different results from others, you have to be willing to do different things than others do and think differently than others think. The reality is most professionals are operating their business based on assumptions (and you know what they say about another name for a donkey and assuming). They, like many of us did at one time, believe the only way to grow a successful company is to work lots of extra hours. They wear "all-nighters" and "hustle and grind" culture like a badge of honor.

I did this. Proudly. But now I know better. Now that I know it is possible to grow an uber-successful, award-winning, impact-driven business that has been named one of the fastest growing in the nation and still be a present parent, spouse, friend, and even have time for fitness and fun (sometimes one in the same, but not always because I've never once called my daily pushups fun). I realize that this "hustle and grind" badge was really a badge of stupidity. Yeah, I said it. And I mean it. It is my greatest desire that when you finish reading this book, you will feel the exact same way.

Throughout this book you will see mentions of "Power Thinking" and what it means to be a "Powerful Professional." In this way, you can start to think differently, act differently, and even dream differently so you can get different results than others do.

This is my mission in life: to save as many professionals as possible from the trials and tribulations of believing they have to work themselves into the ground to achieve their dreams while never managing to reach them.

Now that you have picked up and are actually reading this book, you are already doing things differently. You are a **Powerful Professional.** Here's a sneak peek at what you will discover in the pages that follow, kicking things off with **The Powerful Professionals Motto**:

Powerful Professionals don't make excuses. *They make things happen.*

Powerful Professionals are in control of their business. They are not victims. If something needs to change, they don't dream that it will be different. *They make it different.*

Powerful Professionals know they were not created to fail. They were created to thrive, and success is the greatest response to those who told them they can't. *They don't get even; they get ahead.*

Powerful Professionals choose to surround themselves with those who *inspire, encourage, and empower.*

Powerful Professionals recognize there is an *abundance* of business to be had. They choose whom to work with instead of others choosing to work with them, and they joyfully say "no" to cheap jerk faces.

Powerful Professionals are not distracted by the latest shiny object. They are focused on proven strategies that fit in their sweet spot of gifts and talents.

Powerful Professionals know that their passions are not an accident. They are God-given superpowers.

Powerful Professionals do not waste a dollar out of their pocket, minute of their time, or ounce of their talent. Yet they can't invest fast enough in the tools they need to get them to where they want to go.

Powerful Professionals *do not compromise* on things most important to them. They are flexible in their "how" but never flexible in their "why." Family is not a distraction but a driving force.

Powerful Professionals know that success doesn't always happen on the first try or second or even the third. But success is *inevitable* to those who keep trying. They don't give up when things get hard. *They push harder.*

Powerful Professionals don't wish for change. *They are the change.*

I am a Powerful Professional. And so are you. Keep reading to discover more of what it means to be a Powerful Professional and—more importantly—how to make this way of doing business possible for you.

# POWER GOALS

## Having an Empire Business and Lifestyle Business at the Same Time

**IT WAS A** Tuesday, and the event room was full. As my intro video played, I waited for the moment when Kevin O'Leary from NBC's *Shark Tank* would share that I am his go-to person for monetizing social media.

I scanned the audience to see their reactions. (You learn more looking at the audience than you ever will looking at the video screen.) Eyes were opened, "wow" was mouthed, and several people sat up straighter. More than a few pens were picked up with anticipation for what I would say next. Yes! I thought to myself. *This intro video did its job. Again.*

I proceeded to take the stage, thank the event organizer, give my standard signature speech about scaling business profitably, and then head to the back of the room to chat with those to whom my talk was geared—successful business owners looking to scale.

Or at least that was my goal.

The first one to reach the back of the room was Sonja, who shared that my microphone was still on. "Oh, I know. Thank you." (Sonja didn't realize that this was on purpose to build authority in the room as others listened in to me answering questions.) I had confused Sonja. Bless her heart.

The next person to join me was Tom—mid-50s, great looking suit. He owned a marketing agency and wanted to scale the way I just shared that I had. He wanted to know if he could hire me to show him how to do it. Of course. I gave Tom my email address. No, I don't carry business cards, and that is also on purpose. I told him to shoot me a message, and I'd send him a link to an upcoming event we were holding.

The next person was Roger who worked in the trades and had a big online following but had never monetized it. He was moved by a story I shared on stage, which is what I hear most often during these discussions at the back of the room. It was a true story that connects well with my target audience.

You see, Roger had just heard me share that in my first business, I didn't have boundaries and I worked *all of the time*. I even employed a full-time live-in nanny (call me Ms. Fancy Pants, thank you very much). Except I was always getting sick from being too run down. Social interactions with friends didn't exist except on rare occasions.

I worked constantly, justifying it always. *I need to make more impact. I need to support my family. I need... I need...*

It was a lot of excuses, and frankly I didn't know any better. After all, I had grown up in a house where working harder was the only way to make more money. My father worked three jobs at a time to provide for our family. That's what I knew. I was simply repeating the cycle, always so proud of how hard I could work while everything else fell apart.

One night back then, as I was putting my daughters to sleep and praying over them, I called out to God and prayed, "Can we just freeze time, so I don't miss these girls growing up?"

I wasn't expecting a response. If I'm honest, it was one of those almost rhetorical wishes. Well, be careful what you pray for because sometimes God (or the universe) speaks back.

I heard, *"I don't have to freeze time, Kim. You just have to be more present."*

Ouch. But it was true. I thought I had to work all of the time to keep things going, yet that couldn't have been further from the truth. Working harder was never going to scale my business or give me the life I so desperately wanted. Working more wasn't making things better. It just kept making things worse. Crazily, I kept doing this for more and more time.

But not after that night. I knew then that something needed to change. So when I sold my first company, I committed to setting up my next business in a way that would allow it to scale without sacrificing what was important to me: my faith, my family, and my finances.

As the audience had looked at me with anticipation, I shared the spoiler alert... *it worked!*

From a need so deep it basically filled my soul, I created a system that allowed me to eliminate one-on-one work and scale our business with more profit and more impact. Within one year of implementing this change, my company went from serving 32 clients to over 11,000.

I emphasized it again for those in the back row. *Over 11,000.*

In that same first year, our revenue tripled from what we ever brought in at the previous agency, while still allowing me to be more present, never missing one of my children's monumental moments again.

I had discovered the formula to become a Powerful Professional—one who had both an empire business and a lifestyle business at the same time—growing a super successful, high-impact, purpose-driven company, while maintaining a life I love. Defined by *Forbes Magazine*, a *lifestyle business* is one where you make just enough to support yourself while having more freedom to do the things you *really* want. An *empire business* is one that "has scaled to reach many and massive profits."

A Powerful Professional has both.

At that point, I had made eye contact across the audience and shared, that there is more good news. This is a strategy that has worked again and again, not just for me but for the many clients I've helped, like:

**Todd Tramonte**, who started coaching other realtors on how he became one of the top agents in all of Texas and still takes Fridays off for date days with his wife;

**Maureen Edwards**, who went from selling a few courses at $36 to increasing her course price to $1,000 and launching a high-ticket mastermind;

**Michelle Plucinksy** who scaled her glass-making studio to become one of the top-performing artisans in the country, not only with sales from her core business but now profiting from others seeing how she does her craft;

And **Michael Jaczewski** who scaled his PI business to over $5M in revenue while finally taking time to vacation with family.

It is all about setting non-negotiable boundaries and building your business around them so you can serve your clients and customers without sacrificing what's important.

Roger understood this message because he felt that same yearning. He went right from that cold intro to joining my elite-level mastermind at $40,000.

And so did Samantha.

Clint and Jessica joined the Inner Circle level at $25,000.

And so did Brian.

I generated over six figures of profit from a 45-minute talk with no sales pitch.

How?

When I spoke, it was like I was reading the minds of my perfect prospects. They were then magnetically drawn to me, and they asked to buy. No selling required.

So how can you do this, too? You are about to find out. In this book you will discover how to:

→ Set your Power-thinking non-negotiables that will become the foundation of how your business serves clients, customers, or patients.

→ Identify your right-fit client, customer, or patient whom you were created to serve and who woke up today wanting what you have to offer.

→ Create an offer to serve your market's needs and utilize your greatest strengths that were given to you with a purpose.

→ Establish yourself as the authority, celebrity, and expert in your niche so you become the go-to source for your service.

➡ Build the ultimate impact and income multiplier and bring it to market without sacrificing your health, family, or self.

➡ Discover the secret to scaling in less time by multiplying your time, money, and impact.

Ultimately, you will discover how to scale that time, money, and impact without sacrificing what is important—the ultimate in the "non-hustle-and-grind" way of impact and income multiplication.

You *can* have it all, but not by doing it the way that others have. You must do it in the way you are uniquely called to do.

Ready to find out how? Keep reading.

# 02

# POWER WHYS

## And How They Create Your Bottom Line

**THE CRAZY THING** about driving is if you just get in your car and start going with no idea of where you want to go or why, you will be disappointed by where you end up. So, too, is the case when it comes to growing a successful business. If you don't know why you are building it or what your end goal is, how can you possibly reach your destination?

There is a two-tiered approach I use to walk our clients through this process. It starts with the Money "Why" and then moves forward with creating your non-negotiable boundaries. So first, let's talk money.

## THE MONEY, HONEY

When it comes to your Money Whys there are three questions to answer:

1. How much revenue do you want to generate?
2. How do you want to use this money?
3. Why is this important to you?

For example, I have three main Money Whys:

1.  **My kids.** I want to be able to say "yes" without hesitation to opportunities that come into my children's world, like saying "yes" to attending Nike Basketball Camp, saying "yes" to the softball All-Stars travel team, and "yes" to treating their class to donuts because testing week is over.

    I want to travel with them around the world because through experiencing other cultures, our ignorance dissolves and understanding flourishes. I did not step onto foreign soil until well into adulthood. My children have already dined in the Eiffel Tower, enjoyed tea at Buckingham Palace, and swam off the coast of countries I never heard of before planning these adventures.

    Oh, and momma is no longer sitting at the back of the plane, if you know what I mean. I did that for far too long, and I'm not doing it again. So these trips are not cheap, but they are oh-so important.

    My children are experiencing a bigger world earlier than I was able to, and I am delighted for what this may bring for them in the future and allow them to do moving forward. Call me bougie all you like but fulfilling my children's dreams as they grow and funding first-class international travel are two of my big Money Whys.

2.  **My team.** It is important to me that I do not do anything in my job that I suck at, or that I hate doing. Whatever is not my jam is probably someone else's. I can only truly serve my clients if I work in my unique Zone of Genius. My COO Kelly LeMay's Zone of Genius is breaking down my big vision into smaller tasks so we can get it done. She loves doing this. I hate doing this. It makes sense that she does these things, and I don't. Plus, in order to serve as many people as possible, I need a team to help. Of course they need to be talented and pretty cool folks if I am going to spend time with them—and good, talented people

are not inexpensive hires. My goal is to make enough money to fund a rockstar team of very cool people who multiply our impact every single day. While writing this book, the makeup of my team was…

I can't wait to see how this team grows as we continue to scale.

3. **Giving at will.** When I see a need, I want to be able to give without worrying about it. When things shut down a few years ago and the church I had attended for years needed to find a way to go virtual, I was able to just ask them, "How much do you need?" and write a check to fund their equipment purchase without a second thought.

   During the annual "Buy a Valentine for a Friend" campaign at my daughter's school, I wanted everyone to feel seen, heard, and loved, so I bought one for every child in the school. I heard from teachers that this made the kids beyond happy to have "finally received one this year." To me, nothing is better than spreading joy.

   Giving beyond my tithe of 10 percent is one of my important Money Whys, and I know how much revenue I need to generate in order to make that possible, so this goes into my yearly planning. Your money journey is your own, so you may want to be able to set aside funds to give to your local food pantry, animal shelter, or college alma mater.

# ⏻ POWER EXERCISE

Throughout this book you will find "Power Exercises" for quick wins to implement right away.

Let's start with a quick list of your Money Whys. Fill in this chart with your money priorities. Then list the amount and why it is important.

## TOP THREE MONEY PRIORITIES

| PRIORITY | REVENUE | WHY I WANT IT |
|---|---|---|
| Retirement | Save $100k/y  Live on $250/y | Exit Strategy  Ease + Independence  in dotage |
| Travel | $150k/y | To see the world  before I die |
| Family | $50k/y | To ease their way |
| **TOTAL GOAL** | $550 k/year | |

*Begin with the end in mind—"Show me the money!"*

## ADDING A ZERO

At each of our workshops, we go through the above exercise with clients to lay out their money priorities. Typically, if this is the first time they've allowed themselves to dream about what they really want, they think pretty small. Their idea of "realistic" has been tainted by years of trying to accomplish something but not attaining it. This limitation has been forced upon their dreams for the future. The good news is these are all just thoughts and they can be changed once challenged. So in fact, I challenge them to *add a zero*.

Add a zero to whatever total revenue goal you came up with when you added all of your money priorities together. Make that your new goal to work toward as you lay out your plan to make the big shift in this book.

After all, dreaming big is the only way to make big dreams come true.

While you will be tempted to skip over this strategy and move to the next chapter (weird how I just read your mind, huh?), setting your money goal before building out the plan to achieve it is a vital step in creating a shift plan that is right for you.

I know this requires you to go against common thinking that only seeks immediate pleasure. But since you are reading this book, you are in the top 1 percent of all humans, so we already know you aren't normal. You do things other won't.

It is your time to prove it. Do the work now to reap the benefits later and complete your Power Exercise. Then go back in and add a zero!

## BEYOND THE MONEY: SETTING YOUR NON-NEGOTIABLES

Back when I ran my first company—a marketing agency—I prided myself on responding to every client within one hour, seven days a week. It was a selling point for becoming my client. If you requested to meet with me about your account, the answer was always a resounding "yes" and there was never a wait. Regardless of who you were, if you were willing to hire my company, we would take you on as long as your credit card would successfully process the payment.

These working principals meant that I had no life. I never slept. I was always tethered to my phone and always a ball of stress. Several clients were mean to my team, and I didn't enjoy working with some of them. Eventually, I dreaded going to work at all.

Yet, I couldn't fire myself.

It was not quite the dream I had of owning my own business. I am not mad at the old me. I didn't know any better. But I do now, and you are about to as well.

### SETTING MY NON-NEGOTIABLES BACK THEN

I realized that I was allowing my prospects and clients to have all of the power in the relationship, and I was leaving my future up to them. Like a bad dating relationship (yeah Jim, I'm looking at you), when you give up all of your power, you have a lower perceived value to others. It

*TRUTH!*

was time to get on my "I'm expensive and worth every freaking penny" non-negotiables.

I started by no longer booking any prospect appointment request sooner than 48 hours out. Experts are busy and their time is limited. They aren't waiting around to meet with a prospect; they've got lot of "experty" things to do.

I also stopped sending the prospect to my Calendly where there were 498 open time slots. (Again, successful, highly paid people are busy.) Instead, my prospects were emailed three suggested times to meet by my assistant.

No assistant? No problem. Start with a virtual assistant like Fancy Hands. For only $17 per month you can have someone book appointments for you.

Next, it was time for me to deal with the non-negotiables of creating a better work-life balance. No longer was I going to pride myself on "we get back to you in one hour" philosophies that were complete baloney. If you hire the top advisor in the world, do you really expect them to be on-demand at your will? No way, Jose. You expect to have limited access.

We let our clients know they could continue to contact us on evenings and weekends, but we would not be responding then. Instead, we would only respond Monday through Friday during normal working hours. And I stuck to it. If I wanted to reply on the weekend, I scheduled the email so that it didn't send until the work week started up again.

And one of the biggest changes we made was that cheap jerk-faces could no longer work with us. We would not negotiate on price (more on that in the following chapters), and if someone was mean to my team or me in the sales process or in ongoing client relationships, we would inform them that another marketing consultant was about to be blessed because we weren't the right fit.

Amazingly, as soon as we implemented these changes, the number of requests for prospect appointments went up and our sales increased.

Just like the newest tech gadget or limited-edition Nikes that are hard to get, the more exclusive and limited your time is, the higher its perceived value.

## MY NON-NEGOTIABLES TODAY

When I sold my first company and got the incredible opportunity to start over, I was able to do things right, just like I did the second time I got married.

We set up our company to no longer serve one-on-one clients, establishing clear communications with those who joined our coaching program.

Here are a few ground rules we set right away:

1. You cannot meet with my team or myself without an appointment. Even top clients have to book a time to get me on the phone, and that appointment will always be at least 48 hours out.
2. We do not respond on evenings or weekends. Our clients fully adapted to this working formula, so much so that when they do send messages on evenings or weekends they always start with, "I know you won't get back to me until Monday..."
3. If you are not nice, you cannot be a member of our program. Kindness for the win, always.
4. My team and I have off all holidays, half-day Fridays all summer, and a long break each Christmas holiday. When we are off, we are off.
5. Speaking of my team, everyone does what they are good at and is not asked to perform other people's roles. Including me. I do not spend time doing work I suck at or hate doing. My passions are not an accident; they are my God-given superpowers.
6. We don't work on Sundays and will not host events for our clients that day either. It's a day of rest and renewal.
7. I pray over my members and talk about God's role in my purpose. You are welcome regardless of who you worship (or if you don't at all), but I will mention who is my guiding force.
8. Speaking of the who—our mission is for all to feel heard, seen, respected, and to know they matter, regardless of where they live, the color of their skin, how much money is in their bank

account, how they worship, or who they love. You have to treat others this way as well or you don't belong in our community.

So, what are your non-negotiables?

## ⏻ POWER EXERCISE

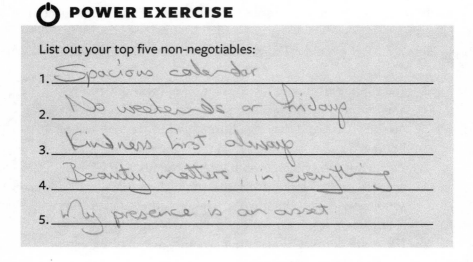

List out your top five non-negotiables:

1. Spacious calendar
2. No weekends or Fridays
3. Kindness first always
4. Beauty matters, in everything
5. My presence is an asset

In the next chapter you will discover how to map out all of your priorities to work together without needing a daily IV of Starbucks (although that does sound delicious) to make it happen.

# POWERFUL PLANNING

## The Five North Stars to Success (aka The Thing You Want to Skip Over But Is Here On Purpose, So Read It Anyway)

**WE'VE GOT WORK** to do. But first, let's celebrate. You have already achieved success just by making it to this page of the book. You are in the minority of all humans and deserve to be celebrated. You've done good.

**You have chosen to thrive.**

Holy cheese and crackers! I am excited for you. You see, this book was made just for you. Because you were made to thrive. *Thrive*, not just in your day, but throughout your whole life.

A continual commitment takes discipline, which isn't easy. That's why most won't do it. *But you aren't most, are you?* You desire more and are willing to do what others won't, which is why you can live a life that most can never dream about. You are a rockstar. Feel free to strum a little air guitar just to celebrate this moment.

**Your time is now.**

It is time to rise above the chaos of "now" and instead do something meaningful. It is time to crush your gigantic, very incredible, and astonishing dreams for your future.

*Because you can. (100 percent.)*

But you can only reach your final destination after you know where you want to go. We all understand that. But do we live it? Are we working toward our future every day?

As you begin to set intentions for what you want your anti-hustle life to be, don't look only at what you want to change, or resolutions you want to make. Set your overall destination for your future based on smaller goals that you can accomplish each day in order to make your very real big dream come true. We call these our North Stars.

## NAMING YOUR NORTH STAR

Here's how I identify my own North Stars. I go through a strategic planning process (aka dreaming up my next goals) every year. It has allowed me to become a better boss, a better mom, and a better wife. It allowed me to become a best-selling author multiple times and to lose 50 pounds (hello, skinny jeans!). I led my marketing firm from bankruptcy to being a multimillion-dollar agency while taking more time off to spend with my husband and glitter-obsessed daughters as well as friends who take me out for wine and make me laugh when I need it most.

This stuff isn't just theory. It works.

Can you achieve all this, just by focusing on big-dream goals? Yes, every day. But the process isn't magic. (Believe me, if there was a magic way, I would have found it and I'd be selling it by now.) The process focuses on outcomes first, then you outline the steps needed to make that outcome a reality.

**It is time. Start here.**

# ⏻ POWER EXERCISE

Go to a quiet place where you feel inspired. It may be your favorite comfy chair, or on a mountain hike, or at the water's edge.

Plan at least 30 minutes of uninterrupted quiet time to complete all steps.

## SET THE DREAM

Picture yourself 10 years from now. **What do you want your life to look like?**

| | |
|---|---|
| Where are you living? | High Rise 3 bed flat near kids Second nest somewhere warm |
| Who is living with you? | w Malcolm ♡ |
| What does an ideal day look like? | Rise when we wake, exercise, At desk @ 10 – 4, dinner + evening together |
| What do you look like physically? | yoga – 130lbs + strong Skin is groomed + nails tended |
| What is your family makeup? | Same as now |
| How much money are you bringing in each month to support your lifestyle? | $100k + |

## Next, amplify your strengths:

| | |
|---|---|
| Of all of the things you do right now as part of your job, what do you enjoy doing most? | Live performances Coaching |
| What do others come to you for advice for? | Glamour Nesting Reinvention |
| What are you best at? | Helping others become their FS |

## Uncover what matters:

| | |
|---|---|
| What is your why? Why do you do what you do? | Because it makes the world a better place (People are happy, creative, accomplished) |

## Bring it all together:

| | |
|---|---|
| Focus on your why, on your financial goals, and on what you are most passionate about. What do you want to accomplish in your career ten years from now? | Best Selling book/s Signature pgm Donate — pg A few 1:1 or a MM $book/year. |

## What that in hand, reverse engineer steps to get from that future back to today:

| | |
|---|---|
| What do you need to have done five years from now to make your ten-year goal possible? | One book<br>Signature pgm<br>Elevation pgm<br>1:1 $300k |
| What do you need to have done one year from now to make your five-year goal possible? | One book<br>Signature pgm<br>1:1 $100k |
| What do you need to have done during the first quarter of the year to make your one-year goal possible? | Book<br>Pgm<br>$25k |
| What do you need to ~~have done this January~~ month to make your quarterly goal possible? | Complete STAR |
| What do you need to have done this week to accomplish your monthly goal? | Recording done |
| What do you need to do today to make this week's goal possible? | Plan week + Follow through |

## Now, it's time to plan your North Stars:

| NORTH STAR GOALS | What do you need to have done five years from now to make your ten-year goal possible? |
|---|---|
| Business | |
| Family | |
| Personal | |
| Spiritual | |
| Health | |

| NORTH STAR GOALS | What do you need to have done one year from now to make your five-year goal possible? |
|---|---|
| Business | |
| Family | |
| Personal | |
| Spiritual | |
| Health | |

| NORTH STAR GOALS | What do you need to have done during the first quarter of the year to make your one-year goal possible? |
|---|---|
| Business | |
| Family | |
| Personal | |
| Spiritual | |
| Health | |

| NORTH STAR GOALS | What do you need to have done this January to make your quarterly goal possible? |
|---|---|
| Business | |
| Family | |
| Personal | |
| Spiritual | |
| Health | |

| NORTH STAR GOALS | What do you need to have done this week to accomplish your monthly goal? |
|---|---|
| Business | |
| Family | |
| Personal | |
| Spiritual | |
| Health | |

| NORTH STAR GOALS | What do you need to do today to make this week's goal possible? |
| --- | --- |
| Business | |
| Family | |
| Personal | |
| Spiritual | |
| Health | |

**Write it down.**

You may be tempted just to "think through" these steps and not write them down, but science tells us to do otherwise. A study by Harvard Business Review shared that people are five times more likely to achieve their goals when they write them down.

**5X your results now by writing down your goals.**

You get to decide. Choose what happens next!

And if you want to be really bold, snap a picture and share your chart on social media using #Powerfulprofessionals.

My amazing, incredible, fabulous reader... you were made to thrive. You weren't made to have your time wasted, your money wasted, or your future wasted. You were meant to flourish and prosper. You were meant to love and be loved. You have a future dream that is yearning for you to get there. You get to decide what to do today. You know now that it will impact what happens tomorrow. You can choose what happens next.

As you go through this book, build these strategies into planning your "next steps," knowing that fulfilling all of your North Stars is not just something you can do, but that you will do.

In the next chapter we'll dive into how to find the audience that can't wait to help you accomplish your North Star goals.

# 04

# POWERFULLY SIMPLE

## The Apex Accelerator
## (How to Easily Fill Your Business with Clients You Love Working With)

**OKAY, THIS IS** not scientific, because there were only a dozen people in the meeting at the time. But before one of our Inner Circle Mastermind sessions, I chatted with early-bird attendees on Zoom. I asked to tell me their "origin stories" of how they joined our coaching program.

Every single one of them was different.

One joined after attending an event. One had been in a lower tier of membership and ascended. One entered straight from a course. Another met me in a different program. One heard me speak at an event.

And so on... No two had the same story.

The one commonality was that they all came into what I call our "Apex Accelerator" and were given a clear path to achieve their goals and knew this was exactly what they were looking for. So they joined. It was like the exact right fit for their business growth goals.

In fact, our "Apex Accelerator" model is the exact thing we used to quickly scale Powerful Professionals—named one of the fastest growing companies by *Inc.* magazine—while still giving me time to catch my children's softball games and be there for moments that matter. It is all about simplification and focusing on a clear path to drive leads and produce sales. Let's see what that looks like in action.

## THE ANATOMY OF THE APEX ACCELERATOR

Our entire business model can fit in on a napkin. It looks like this:

In the next several chapters, we will break down each step of this Apex Accelerator, but first I want to give you an overview along with a few examples of what this can look like for different situations. The shape is a fat triangle with steps up the side that you lead your prospect along a defined path.

The first step starts by attracting prospects. You can use free content like blogs, emails, podcasting, organic social media posts, and speaking on stage, as well as paid advertising to bring someone in via a free gift offer you may have promoted online.

The next step is to invite that person to a webinar. The offer made during the webinar will be for them to purchase a course. That course sale funds the rest of the Apex Accelerator growth as it attracts your right-fit clients and in turn funds all of your marketing. It is the Ultimate Client Generation Machine. (More on that in Chapter 6.)

With the course purchase comes a ticket to a virtual event. During the virtual event you can make an offer for a group coaching program, like our Power Up Accelerators Club. About 30 percent of those who come from the course will take that offer.

While in the Power Up Accelerators Club, our members are introduced to the Inner Circle Mastermind and about 30 percent move up to that level. And while in Inner Circle, members are introduced to the Elite level, and again, about 30 percent move up to that.

Why 30 percent? I don't know, but it works out that way and my favorite quote is, "In God I trust. All others bring data," so that is just how the numbers work out.

Being so clear about the journey of membership allows my team and me to go deep on the marketing and messaging, figuring out (with measurable data) what works best and what doesn't work at all. We can do this because we aren't crafting brand new promotions or launching new products, programs, and services every week. We are focused on exactly what our prospects need.

Now, you may run a more traditional consulting or professional services business like my client Jeffrey Rehmeyer. He is an attorney, and his structure looks like this:

1. He hosts a weekly show where he interviews different experts on Estate Planning topics, broadcast simultaneously to Facebook, LinkedIn, and YouTube.
2. He boosts those videos to reach more people.
3. He retargets those who watch the videos to attend his webinar.
4. On the webinar he shares why they need to make Estate Planning changes now, depending on the age of their children.
5. Once the prospect becomes an Estate Planning client, he works with them on other relevant areas of law.

One of our past agency clients, Mode, is a medical spa that typically brings in clients for one treatment, then enrolls them in a subscription and later engages them in additional services. Their Apex Accelerator looks like this:

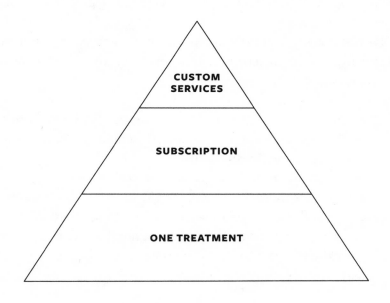

One of my private clients, Chris Gronkowski, uses a similar model for his product-based business—an ice shaker for protein shakes. He draws customers to a video where he sells a course and offers his product on the thank-you page.

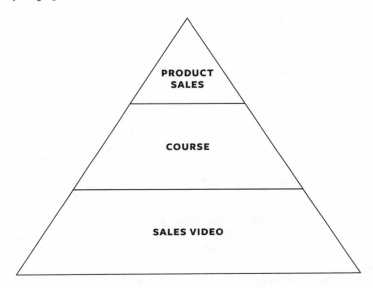

Whatever your current business model is right now, challenge your brain to conceptualize how the Apex Accelerator can work for you.

We've included a cheat sheet to draft yours out in the Powerful Professional Book Bonus Bundle that's yours for free at TheShiftBookBonus.com.

## WHAT ABOUT THE MONEY WHYS?

In the last chapter we already dove into identifying your Money Whys, so the question now becomes, "How do you achieve your money goals using this simple model?"

Well, because the model is so simple, it can be very profitable. Here's how we do it (your mileage may differ).

Our course is priced at $1,497. Group Coaching is $14,997. Mastermind is $24,997. Elite Coaching is $40,000.

And 30 percent of members ascend at each level.

I know this to be true: It isn't magic—it's math.

Back when I was launching my first digital course, the only data I had to base my beliefs on was what I saw the "gurus" talking about during their huge launches. So after I held my first launch and only sold three courses during the first webinar, I hired a coach to tell me what I was doing wrong.

It was four o'clock in the afternoon, and I had just paid $600 for a half-hour coaching call with a business guru to guide me through what I thought was a major disaster. My flight had been delayed, not leaving me enough time to catch a cab to my hotel, and my phone was almost dead. So I did what every road warrior has to do in order to get the job done.

I found a spot on the dirty airport floor near an outlet and set up a temporary conference call so I could get that coaching I had paid for.

When the coach answered the phone, we exchanged short pleasantries and then I got right down to it. "Hey, I need help," I apologized. "My launch started today, and the cart is now open, but I've only had three sales. I feel like such a failure."

Remember that for more than 10 years I had run a consulting firm and was getting paid by clients to grow their sales. We only generated sales when I worked directly with clients. No matter how hard I worked, I couldn't manage to generate enough sales to get us out of a cycle of cashflow purgatory. I was tired of waking up every night at 3:00 a.m. in a panic that I was going to overdraw my bank account and miss payroll. This launch was supposed to get me out of that hot-mess express, but it didn't seem to be working.

The coach asked me, "Kim, is this your first launch?"

I replied, "Yup."

"How much is your course?"

"$997," I answered.

"So you made $3,000 today?"

"Yes," I kept apologizing. "I know that is terrible compared to others."

"Compared to who?" he asked.

"Compared to all of the six- and seven-figure launches I see others having," I whined.

"Kim," I heard, followed by a pause. "You can't compare your Chapter 1 with their Chapter 20. You earned $3,000 on Day 1, when most of your sales won't come in until the end. And my guess is that $3,000 is more than you've ever made in one day. You should be celebrating!"

He was right. Three thousand dollars was more than I had ever made in a single day. Before that launch, I had needed to do an entire month's work for a client in order to generate half as much money since our monthly fee was $1,500.

So why was I freaking out?

I realized I had only seen the successes of others from their highlight reel. I didn't know their backstory. I had compared my *start* to their *now* and that wasn't helping anyone. From that point on, I vowed I would be transparent in my storytelling, fact sharing, and highlight-reel showing.

That transparency is something I have stayed committed to. Even after:

➡ Our sales grew and we went on to develop our consulting firm into an asset we could sell;

- ➡ We launched our own coaching business that we'd grown to land on the Inc. 5,000 at #475;
- ➡ I'd been hired by celebrity clients like Kevin O'Leary from *Shark Tank* and television and movie stars, and spoke on stages alongside superstars like Tony Robbins, Grant Cardone, and Emmitt Smith;
- ➡ Sales still soared when I changed my hours so that I could be there for my girls each day as they got off the school bus.

I vowed I would always tell the "we didn't magically get here" part of the story so others would know that no one starts with a list, a follower, or a sale. We all start with zero, but that can change in seconds by taking the next step to start growing that audience, list, and sales.

During that first launch I ended up generating $10,000 in course sales, which covered payroll for the month. I was able to breathe again and recognize that the reason I started that journey in the first place wasn't by accident. It was so my hot mess could become my future message and someone else's miracle. I was always in that right place at the right time.

This is the reason why I always share the "*real* real" and never sugarcoat it.

## WHAT THE NUMBERS REALLY LOOK LIKE

For every 100 people who enroll in our course, 33 become coaching clients in our Power Up Accelerators Club group coaching program, 11 join our Inner Circle mastermind, and three to four will join our Inner Circle Elite level coaching.

**The Math, Not Magic breakdown:**

| | |
|---|---|
| 100 people in course | $149,700 |
| 33 in Power Up Accelerators Group Coaching | $494,901 |
| 11 Inner Circle Mastermind | $274,967 |
| 3 in Inner Circle Elite | $120,000 |
| Every 100 people in course | $1,039,568 |

That's right. For every 100 customers, another seven figures of revenue flows into the business.

So, the question becomes: How do we find those 100 people again and again? And how can you? That is exactly what we'll dive into in the next chapter.

100 into STAR @ $1k $100,000.00
30 into SPOTLIGHT $ 150,000
@ $5k
11 into ?? @ $10k $ 110,00
_____
$360,000 /100 people

# POWERFUL PROSPECTING

## Your Apex Alex and Ally... Giving All Your Attention to Your Right-Fit Client

**IMAGINE A COCKTAIL** party filled with your ideal prospects. You move from group to group enjoying conversation after conversation. Everyone wants to work with you, and they are a joy to talk to. You are sipping on your favorite cocktail or mocktail and feeling energized.

I don't know about you, but in my dream room, there would also be a Tito's bar, a Veuve fountain, and a gorgeous sushi display.

Sounds good, doesn't it? While we may be a bit away from a *Real Housewives*-worthy hosting budget, we can recreate this scenario in our own businesses. It is possible to ensure that everyone you work with, from prospect to top-tier client, is your ideal client. This type of client is an essential component of the shift you can make to a no-hustle scale. And after their first transaction with you, they just keep on doing business. The value of the relationship grows and grows.

### IDENTIFYING THE IDEAL CLIENT

Start from the beginning with identifying exactly who you want to work with. Then your subsequent offers take them up your Apex Accelerator one step after another.

First, imagine the kind of person you want to work with at your top tier. This is your Apex Alex or Ally. Who is this person, and what does this person want? The clearer you can be about who this person is and what they are thinking, desiring, or yearning for, the easier attracting this person becomes.

At first, I thought my target market was anyone running a business and not scaling as fast as they wanted. What I came to realize is that I want to work with people who not only *can* use that information but *will*. I want to work with the impact-makers because they are exactly who the world needs right now.

As I started working with this specific individual, I got even more clear on who they were outside of their company, what they really desired, and what drives them.

My "Alex" is someone who has owned a business for several years, has relied on word-of-mouth marketing and referrals in order to grow, and is frustrated that he hasn't grown faster. He has tried to do some marketing but hasn't gotten the results he wants and is wondering if this can ever actually work for him.

He's wasted time and money trying to grow his business in the past. He works a ton of hours and is exhausted, feeling burnt out. He wants to have more success and to be more present with his family. He thinks of his funeral that will happen someday, and at this moment, he doesn't like what his kids will probably say.

He is a person of action and is into some type of sport. He cycles, does Tough Mudders and Spartan races, or works out. Alternatively (or in addition), he is a frequent flyer with premium status on at least one airline.

He is an ambitious action taker who simply needs to learn how to grow and scale effectively, and he will do it. Right now he simply doesn't know where to start.

My Alex wants to not only generate income but to make a massive impact on the world while reclaiming his time and money freedom.

That is my guy.

Every marketing message I put out into the world, every piece of content I create, and every offering I release is for him. And he hears me clearly through the clutter because I am willing to laser focus on him. Let's take a look at some examples of "Alex" that my clients have come up with:

➡ For our Inner Circle Elite member Todd Tramonte, his "Alex" is a Real Estate agent who is earning about $250,000 and wants to become a 7-figure earner and get time freedom back.

➡ Power Up Member Kim Kiel's "Ally" is a coach who is struggling to market effectively who can't find the right words to write. She makes copywriting fun, easy, and very profitable.

➡ Inner Circle Member Jenny Benzie's "Ally" is a wine shop owner struggling to increase revenue who is overworked and overwhelmed. She shows them how to easily increase their revenue *and profit*.

➡ Inner Circle Members Jan and Monica Zands serve "Ally and Alex." Their prospects are a couple who fight over money a lot. They love each other and want to bring wealth, health, and happiness into their marriage but don't know how. Jan and Monica empower couples to have a relationship rich in love, time, health, and money.

➡ Inner Circle Elite Member Kevin Mar's "Sonali" (his version of Ally), is in high school and struggling with self-esteem. This person wants to feel empowered and part of a community. Kevin unlocks the power of being a fencing champion and the scholarships that come with it.

How about your perfect client? Is it an Alex or Ally, or a Jennifer or Joe? What does this person's life look like right now? What is this person desiring? What problem do they want to fix?

As I ask you, I understand that your brain is most likely totally freaking out thinking, *I can't pick just one! Please don't make me!* (Even throwing in some cute puppy dog eyes for good measure.) You are probably asking yourself: *How can I serve so many when I am being asked to pick just one?*

Well, let me share a few insights...

First, give yourself grace. Your brain is normal, and it is normal to wonder who you will miss out on if you focus exclusively on who you really want to reach.

Second, you are starting with just one but can eventually go after many. This is just the ideal one to start with.

Third, if you don't pick, it is impossible to develop effective marketing. Impossible. You can't directly speak to more than one person at a time. Can I laser focus on you and also laser focus on someone else at the same time? I am one incredibly talented multi-tasker who gets a lot of things done and yet I can still only laser focus on one thing at a time.

By targeting your messaging to your exact right-fit client, this person will hear you through the clutter and noise and come to believe that you are reading their mind.

That is the secret to effectively marketing and scaling: being so clear on your right-fit person that they come to you because they see you as the obvious solution they have been looking for all along.

So how do you figure out who your "Alex" or "Ally" is?

Start by thinking of all of your clients. Who was your favorite? Who found the most success from the work you did together? Who did you most enjoy working with? Who found the most benefit from the work you did together?

Describe that person.

Or maybe it is someone you'd love to land as a future client. Who are they? What is going on in their life right now? What do they want for their future? Describe them.

Or if you are just not sure, start with *you*, three years ago. What did you want? What problem did you desire to solve? How did you solve it? Pick one of these and make this your Apex "Alex" or "Ally," or whatever name you choose.

If you are still having a hard time choosing just one, think of this scenario. You are sitting in first class on a plane from Atlanta to New York, a flight I do often. It lasts one hour and 45 minutes and there is one open seat next to you. The two people you most desire to work with are both on this plane, but only one can sit next to the fabulousness that is you.

You get to pick who is it.

Without a second thought, which one sits down?

This is your "Alex" or "Ally."

Don't second-guess it, for there is no right or wrong answer. In fact, the only thing that could be wrong here is not making a decision.

## ⏻ POWER EXERCISE

With our coaching clients, we've developed an easy method to connect and get more inside of the mind of your Alex. It is called the "Letter from Alex" method, where you write a letter to yourself from this ideal prospect that you will get one year from now.

The letter goes like this:

**Dear** _____ ,
                (YOUR NAME)

**Before I met you I** _____
                    (DESCRIBE WHAT THEIR LIFE WAS LIKE BEFORE)

_____

**Then** _____
      (WHAT CHANGE TOOK PLACE)

_____

**And now my life is** _____

_____

**Thank you for** _____

_____

_____
                (YOUR ALEX'S NAME)

Take the time to write this letter to yourself now and place it somewhere visible as you create your marketing and sales strategies, always keeping your Alex in mind.

For a downloadable copy of the Alex letter, visit TheShiftBookBonus.com to claim your bonus bundle.

Now, how do you get your Alex's attention? Read on!

## HOW TO MAGNETICALLY ATTRACT YOUR ALEX

As I was driving home from a softball game that was night one of a three-day tournament for one of my girls, I stopped at Walgreens to see if something might magically appear that could help make the heat more bearable the next day.

I walked the aisles, appearing like a middle-aged, suburban zombie that came across an oasis. *Could this really be?* Were my eyes deceiving me, or was the solution in front of me right that very second?

It was indeed. I saw an entire display of battery-operated fans that could be used to cool the team members plus myself. I bought all the fans and all the batteries and ended up walking out with my arms full.

The store got my attention because they had exactly what I wanted in that moment. And that is what is required of effective marketing. That's what I call "Power Marketing."

Money-making, game-changing marketing focuses on what your Alex wants, not on what you sell. Not on your process. Not on your program. Not on your service. Not how your Alex is broken. Not even on what your Alex needs.

Power Marketing focuses on what your prospect *wants*.

And it's simpler than you may think. Nail that and everything becomes easier, including scaling your business and making the shift away from the constant hustle.

For example . . .

- ➡ If you are a marketer, your Alex wants more leads/sales.
- ➡ If you are a nutritionist, your Alex wants weight loss.
- ➡ If you sell swag, your Alex wants more sales and/or employee satisfaction and high performance.
- ➡ If you are a relationship coach, your Alex wants to find love and stay in it.

→ If you are an IT professional, your Alex wants nothing to interrupt doing business and making money.

What does your market want?

And do not say "confidence," "to become unstuck," or to "find purpose." *Everyone* wants that. This is not specific. Plus it is a feeling—not an outcome.

## ⏻ POWER EXERCISE

Challenge yourself to complete this sentence:

**My Alex wants** _____

**so that my Alex can** _____ .

**The "so that they can…" is the money sentence.**

Keep adding on to this phrase to narrow down the big idea that will attract your perfect client. If your brain is screaming, "But I want to talk about…" (insert the thing that you want to talk about) with your prospect, instead of the thing they want, then ask yourself this question:

**Am I willing to put my ego behind my mission?** Because effective marketing focuses on what your prospect wants, not on what you want to talk about.

Once you bring in your prospect as a client and start working together, you will be able to work on many different things. The secret is getting their attention in the first place. You can never accomplish that by focusing on you or what you want.

Here is an example of "what not to do" based on a vacation experience:

Years ago, The Tall One (aka my husband Ian) and I got into cruising. I'm not sure how this happened. Perhaps it was the drink package and large Coca-Cola thermos? Always "going big or going home," we hit the highest-level rewards status with Royal Caribbean (RC). Because of this, we were invited to a few special events during the cruise. I love going to these, not because of the cheap champagne or cheese displays, but because of the marketing behind them.

One of the night's events was an awards ceremony with a twist. RC celebrates its customers for having spent money with them. They literally give out awards on every cruise to the three people with the most "points." These are only earned through going on cruises, so we were there cheering for those who were the most loyal customers.

Following the awards, they brought out the "Next Cruise Specialist" (a sales guy) to talk about some of the exciting cruise options we could now book. They reward and create significance for their community and encourage them to spend more money. Effective marketing makes it all about the client.

That's great in theory. However, human error can mess things up!

When the Captain came up to greet us all, he shared that he's been cruising for 16 years, but never as a guest. He went on to say that if he did ever go on one, it wouldn't be Royal Caribbean because he's seen too much.

(Way to make everyone in the room who had spent tens of thousands with this company feel special.)

Then the Next Cruise Specialist got up and shared some feature-based reasons to cruise. He ended by trying to be funny. "We speak three languages: Mastercard, Visa, and American Express."

Yes, the crowd laughed. But he ruined the sale. Why? Because he made it about the purchase, not about the experience. He focused on his ego rather than his audience. The captain had done the same thing. His desire to seem superior outweighed his desire to be effective.

These people aren't alone. Business owners do this all of the time. They make their messaging about them. They go for clever over clear. They care more about their status than their community.

Your Alex or Ally must come first. Always.

Show your appreciation. Let them know they made a brilliant decision to pay attention to your marketing, to opt-in for your free gift, and to work with you. Let them know they are among other brilliant people who did the same. Tell them they are significant and show them they matter and that you are so proud they chose you. And that if you were buying, you would choose you, too.

You are amazing and deserve to be treated that way. So do your prospects and customers.

RC got that wrong, and my guess is, it cost them thousands. Multiplied by ego-driven captains and sales professionals, this behavior could cost them millions if not billions. When you launch your marketing, keep your market in mind.

Want to see some great examples of how to keep your market in mind? Head on over to the book bonus at TheShiftBookBonus.com and check out the case studies! How will you reach your amazing Alex and Ally? In the next chapter, we dive into exactly that.

# POWERFUL LEAD GENERATION

## Creating an Endless Supply of Quality Leads

**NOW THAT YOU** know who your Alex or Ally is, where do you find them and get their attention? In this chapter we will dive into many lead-generation strategies, starting first with social media because there are billions of people there, waiting to buy from you.

And they are all currently thinking, "I want to get on Facebook so I can buy stuff."

Hardly.

Often people head online to be entertained and inspired. If you want to leverage the power of social media, you can't show up with a sale. The same is true for any type of marketing. Approach your prospect with value first and the sale second.

Besides people who get drunk in Vegas, no one wants to get married on the first date.

Instead, follow **M.O.M.—Magnet, Opt-in, Monetize**.

- **Magnet:** First, magnetically attract your perfect prospect with a message focused on solving their problem. Prospects should know right away who you serve and why they should care.
- **Opt-in:** Shift the lead off social media as fast as possible (or whatever channel you may be in), away from cute kitten videos and funny memes by offering a free gift in exchange for the opt-in. For example, something that gives a quick win—like a list of tools they can use—works great. Even better, give away a free course or training that doesn't pitch anything but gives them a chance to get to know you right away. This will lead them to say, "Wow, that is so good and it's free! I wonder what the paid stuff is like!"
- **Monetize:** Monetize your offer on the thank-you page by selling something or booking an appointment. Only 5-10 percent of your possible customers will be ready to buy, but these amazing folks will fund your marketing. For the rest, you've now got their contact information, so you'll follow up for when they are ready to buy later.

Remember: magnetically attract by giving value, get the opt-in, and then monetize. After all, M.O.M. knows best.

## HELPING YOUR CLIENT MEET M.O.M.

Begin the M.O.M. process with your "magnet." The magnet is the free gift you will offer. It should focus on what the prospect really wants. Start by solving one problem your target client has and offering value for free, up front.

Like...

**"5 Ways to_____ (outcome)
without _____ (something they don't want to do)"**

Examples . . .

- ➡ 5 Ways to Make Money with Your Cell Phone When You Don't Yet Have a List
- ➡ 5 Ways to Become a Best-Selling Author When You Don't Have a Big Following
- ➡ 5 Ways to Boost Your Metabolism Without Giving Up Foods You Love
- ➡ 5 Ways to Scale your Business Without Sacrificing Everything That's Important to You

Write out your five tips first as bullets.

Next, use Zoom or another video app to create a video where you guide your prospect through the five ways. This video becomes your free gift that you can now call a "free course" to attract your right-fit client.

If you have trouble coming up with a topic, a great resource is answerthepublic.com. It is a collection of searches people make online about your topic area that will show you what your market is already interested in learning about.

An example of this type of free gift offer is one we have set up at **theaudiencebuilderblueprint.com**.

I put together a free course, walking you through five ways to utilize free social media tactics to generate leads, grow your audience, and get more clients without spending money on advertising, aka exactly what my target market wants.

**Audience Builder Blueprint Opt-in page (from theaudiencebuilderblueprint.com)**

With the Magnet and Opt-in in place, the next step is to Monetize. This is the offer you will put on your thank-you page for claiming your free gift. There is no right or wrong here, just options, and we use all of them because different people respond to different offers.

Here are some options for your thank-you page offer:

1.  **Book an appointment:** If your offering is over $3,000 and/or requires an ongoing relationship, then you would be best served to send the prospect to a conversation with you. I don't fancy saying, "It's a strategy session," because to me, this feels like trickery and the worst way to start a client relationship. Instead, be very straight forward and tell the prospect, "You are booking this call to find out if you want to become a client so that we can give you what you want faster."

Script for video:

*Hello there! Thanks for opting in to get the Audience Builder Blueprint so you can generate more leads. And since you did request that, I know something to be true about you.*

*You see, my name is Kim Walsh Phillips, and I've generated over a billion dollars online. I've worked with professionals and clients to grow their businesses. And I know if you download this report, then one of the biggest challenges you are facing is about getting more leads and generating more sales for your business.*

*Chances are, you are looking to scale up in order to multiply your impact and your income, without having to work more hours. Well, I'd love to see how we might be able to help you do exactly that.*

*So, because you downloaded the free report, you've just unlocked the opportunity to get a marketing consultation with one of my business opportunity advisors. You are going to get on the phone with someone who's going to show you where the greatest opportunities for growth are inside your business right now.*

*Maybe it's about getting more leads right away from social media, or maybe it's about automating some of the activities you're already doing, or maybe it's about how to close more of those sales from your one-on-one calls. Well, we can identify exactly what you need right now and see how we might be able to work together in order to accomplish your goals.*

*If you would like to scale your business quickly, make sure to fill out the form below. I know it's a little long. It's because getting this information helps us to know as much as we can about you and how to serve you when we talk.*

*So, fill out the information below and then schedule your call with one of my incredible advisors. They're going to be able to guide you on the fast path to scale your biz!*

*I can't wait to hear about all your success!*

2. **Purchase a digital course:** This can be something you create or something you sell as an affiliate. In one of our free gift funnels, we simply offer a course on Instagram Marketing for $7 on the thank-you page and that offsets the cost of all of our marketing.

**Example: $7 Instagram marketing course**

3. **Purchase an event ticket:** As a sponsor of events, often we cannot sell something, but we can offer a free gift. So, we get a little ninja about it and offer an opt-in to a masterclass on the first page and then offer a ticket to the event on the thank-you page. It works, too. Twelve percent of all who landed on that page took the offer.

**Example: Masterclass opt-in**

4. **Upgrade to VIP:** When we run our once-a-year challenge, "10X Your Business Page Followers," registration is free, but we offer

**Example:** 10X Challenge opt-in

an opportunity to upgrade to VIP on the thank-you page. This not only funds the marketing for the challenge, but it gets the person who joins the challenge to make more of a commitment by making a financial commitment. When people pay, they pay attention.

5. **Confirm a webinar registration and add to calendar:**
   Sometimes the best thing you can do is simply get them to show up at the webinar, so adding your event to their calendar is the most important thing you can do. With that in mind, make the entire thank-you page's purpose to do just that.

No matter what you do, don't just use this page to say "thank you," because you are leaving far too much money on the table if you do.

Keep your M.O.M. formula geared to what your Alex wants. Make it all about value, and then build a relationship before making the sale. This is the best way to attract your right-fit client.

## ⏻ POWER EXERCISE

5 Ways to _____ (outcome)

without _____ (something they don't want to do)

1. _____

2. _____

3. _____

4. _____

5. _____

# LEAD GENERATION MADE EASY

While growing up, I went to school with lots of people who had more money than I did. They wore jeans with the Guess triangle on the back ($80 each in the dark ages, so like $12 million today), carried designer Il Bisonte purses, and had naturally straight hair that didn't require a gallon of White Rain mousse to calm itself down from the clouds (praying no one would actually try to touch my mane because they may cut themselves).

They had all the things that I wanted.

I didn't just wish I had it better. I did something about it. I did what every ambitious young person with more taste than money does. I got a job at Burger King (where they would hire at age 14) and got my tush to work. I made my own money, bought the purse (soft leather, a story for another day), got the jeans, and (thank the wonderful Lord in heaven) found a hairdresser who understood how to tame a curl. I mean, there were no TikTok videos back then showing us how. We actually needed to rely on professionals. I also smelled like grease and needed to shower the second I finished work before I could meet up with friends.

Within six months, I was made assistant manager, but as soon as I turned 15, I landed a better job. Yet I had found a way to get what I wanted. I felt really proud that I had earned all of those things I desired. This is something that has never changed.

There is never an "I can't" for me. There is always an "I can. I just need to figure out how."

When someone asks me, "What is the number-one way I can generate more leads?" I cringe. No offense to those who have asked, but that is really a not-so-clever way to say, "Is there a lazy way to grow my business? Because I'd really like that option."

Yeah, no. That isn't how this works.

When it comes to reaching your target market, the best way is *many ways*. Effective marketing utilizes more than one channel to reach your target market. Next, we will dive into multiple ways to reach your target market that will get you faster results in less time so you get exactly what you want: a business that scales with exact right-fit clients, and that multiplies every minute of your day, each ounce of your talent and energy, and every last ever-loving dollar out of your pocket.

## OPP: OTHER PEOPLE'S PEOPLE

The reality is your audience already exists in someone else's audience. Some of my best clients came from another person's audience. Either I spoke on their stage, they promoted one of my product launches, they spoke at my summit, I was a guest on a podcast, or I participated in some other media or event they had.

## ⏻ POWER EXERCISE

To determine where your audience already exists, start by making a list of 25 people who serve the same people as you do.

1. _____   2. _____

3. _____   4. _____

5. _____   6. _____

7. _____   8. _____

9. _____   10. _____

11. _____   12. _____

13. _____   14. _____

15. _____   16. _____

17. _____   18. _____

19. _____   20. _____

21. _____   22. _____

23. _____   24. _____

25. _____

Next, investigate if these influencers have any of the following:

➡ Do they have a podcast that allows guests?
➡ Do they hold events you can sponsor?
➡ Is there a membership group you can join?
➡ Is there a Facebook group you can be part of?
➡ Something else?

Write all of these down.

| INFLUENCER'S NAME | |
|---|---|
| Podcast? | |
| Events? | |
| Membership? | |
| Facebook Group? | |
| Other? | |

Next, I want you to promote them before you ask them to promote you. Here are a few ways you can do this right away:

➡ If you have a podcast, invite them to be a guest.
➡ Ask to interview them for a Facebook Live that you promote to your list.
➡ Have them as a guest in your Clubhouse room or Twitter Space if you run one regularly.

While I do all of these things, there is a fast path to list growth and developing relationships with future potential partners. It is by holding a summit or livecast event. During this event you will interview speakers on a set topic where they will each offer a bonus to drive toward an action—like buy recordings of the summit, get a ticket to your event, purchase your book, donate to a charity, or buy your course or any other offering you may have.

I've held livecasts for all of these purposes. Each time I've launched a book, such events have brought me to best-selling status easily. In fact, for my last book, the publisher told me all of the print copies sold out within three hours because of that livecast.

Whenever we hold a virtual event, we host a summit the week before where we interview people on the event topic. This drives ticket sales in the door each and every time, on average accounting for 25 percent of all ticket sales in just one day.

Recently we held a virtual event for a charity. I am on their board, and I interviewed other board members and supporters. Together we were able to raise thousands of dollars and grow the organization's list while also bringing more attention to their mission.

Ideas for your summit can include:

- Other "gurus" who serve the same niche
- Peers
- Topic niche
- Location-specific
- Current event
- Subculture

Recruit your speakers from:

- Contact list
- Ask your inner circle to recommend one person
- Second-tier LinkedIn contacts
- Vendors
- Your "dream" ask (more later in this chapter)
- Hire a speaker using a speaking agency
- Recruitment emails (example below)

Here's an example ask and follow-up email you can use to recruit guests for your summit:

Subject: **(Name)**, May I promote you to my audience?

Hi **(Name)**,

I am reaching out to interview you for our upcoming **(name of summit)**. My audience would love to hear about **(name of speaker's topic)**.

I know your time is valuable, so in exchange for you being a guest, I would love to share your website and/or giveaway to our viewers and afterwards on our list.

Of course, we can record the interview at your convenience to make sure the time works for you. And we will create all marketing materials including emails and social media posts to promote your involvement to our list.

All we ask is that you share the event with your list at least once and post it on social media. All of the other speakers will do the same, so you will get even more lead generation opportunities throughout the Summit.

Can we start promoting you as a speaker?

Cheers,

**(Your Name)**

And here's an example follow-up:

Subject: Re: Promoting you to our list.

Hi **(Name)**,

Follow up on my email below. Please let me know if we can start promoting you as a speaker?

**(copy and paste message from above)**

Each speaker promotes the event to their list, introducing you (and them) to more people. To be fair, I don't ask the top-named folks to promote. Instead, I leverage the celebrity of their name to get other speakers.

Here's an example of an email we sent out to prospective attendees promoting a summit:

**(Name),**

What if you could secretly get the blueprint of the most successful names in business? Would you want to take a peek?

Register now for this can't-miss event, and that is exactly what you'll receive.

WANT FLOOD OF RIGHT-FIT CLIENTS COMING TO YOUR DOOR?
BEHIND-THE-SCENES SECRETS FROM THE BIGGEST NAMES IN BUSINESS

**SCALE FAST** LIVECAST

Join us for business-building strategies that will skyrocket your sales without relying on referrals or sacrificing your time. Register now.

Cheers,

Kim "Scaling with the Help of Some of My Friends" Walsh Phillips

To see more examples of invites we have used in emails, on social media, and on our site, visit TheShiftBookBonus.com.

## THE PROSPECT LEAD MACHINE

I suck at a lot of things—like reading fine print, or cooking something with more than five ingredients, or helping with my daughter's fourth-grade math homework. These things are not my jam. But finding ways to make lead generation easy is. And this little funnel is ninja. Running it brings me free, high-quality leads, all day long.

Here's how it works:

1. Allow the house that Zuck built (aka Facebook) to fill up your sales pipeline. Start by setting up your Facebook group for free at facebook.com/groups.
2. All of your prospects woke up today thinking about themselves, not about you, so name your group something that focuses on your perfect target market. Ours is called "Powerful Professionals." A fitness coach client of mine named his group "In High Gear." One of my business coach clients has a group called "Profit & Purpose." Name your group after your right-fit prospects to attract them in.
3. Write your group description to set the tone for some amazing people to join. Here's ours:

> What is the Fast Growth Strategies Group all about?
>
> This group is a safe place to share ideas from a company that actually runs a successful consulting business and has successfully scaled multiple companies. This group is sponsored by Powerful Professionals, so everything here from us is free. Please stay humble, no foul language and encouraging posts only please. Just be cool...
>
> **Must be a business owner to join!**

> We do this because we believe there are a lot of entrepreneurs and small business owners providing incredible service to their clients, but they just don't know how to scale.
>
> If you are a successful professional services provider or run a coaching company, then join in and offer some help! Either way, let's have some fun and raise the bar of this industry. We're not growing our businesses... We're changing an industry and impacting the world!

4. Create member questions to generate leads. You are officially granted my permission to steal ours (see below). I just ask that when you are on the cover of *Forbes* as one of the most influential people in the world, please remember my name and pour a little seltzer on the sidewalk in my honor.

> 1. This group was created for business owners to scale their business. What is the name of your business?
> 2. What is the best email address for you?
> 3. We work with business owners to double their profits. Would you like more information about working with us? If so, please leave your mobile number (xxx-xxx-xxxx) below.

5. Give Facebook the heads up that you should be showing up all over your new prospect's newsfeed. Do this by getting the person to engage right away. How? Add in a welcome post, welcoming them to the group and asking them to introduce themselves.
6. No one likes to enter an empty room, so first invite your team and friends to join your group to set the stage with social proof that "people like this place."

7. Copy the answers to your new members' requests to join so you capture their email. (We use a software that automatically does this for us and adds them to our database. Find out more at TheShiftBookBonus.com.)

Now that you have your empire established, it's time to fill 'er up with quality leads for free. Let's head over to LinkedIn.

1. On LinkedIn, search for your Alex using the free search tools.
2. Save your search by copying the URL result into your notes. You'll be able to turn back to this amazing list whenever you want.
3. Connect with 10 people per day from your search list with the message:
   "Came across your profile here and would love to connect. Cheers, Your Name"
4. When they accept your connection request, endorse their skills.
5. After you do that, shoot them a message that says,
   "So great to connect. I have a free Facebook group about (fill in the blank). I'd love for you to join us. May I send you the link?"
6. When they say "yes," send them the link. (We use a software that automatically does all of this for us and adds them to our database. Find out more at TheShiftBookBonus.com)

You now are connected with your perfect prospects on LinkedIn. You also have them in your Facebook group and will have a potential lead requesting a phone call with you. Game changing!

As an added bonus, see the "Power Thinking vs. Common Thinking" strategy for how to reach your contacts in LinkedIn on autopilot each week, because using LinkedIn and Facebook Groups is just one way we generate more clients. Visit www.TheShiftBookBonus.com for access.

# ⏻ POWER STRATEGY: YOUR BOOK

*By Russell Brunson, founder of ClickFunnels Software*

When I created my company, I wanted to figure out how to get my message to infiltrate and to teach those strategies so others could do the same. But when we first launched ClickFunnels, there was no desire for it. No one knew why they needed a marketing funnel or any of the reasons behind it. The business was not growing, and I had all sorts of problems. Then I wrote my first book, *Dotcom Secrets*.

We sent copies out to many influencers and made a funnel to sell it. Inside the book, I shared all the strategies for how someone would actually use a funnel. People got the book and they read it.

Then more people got the book, read it, and found value. The next logical thing after they understood why they needed a funnel was to come and start using ClickFunnels to build their own marketing using our system and strategies.

Later I wrote another book about how to get your messaging inside of funnels, *Expert Secrets*. My third book is called *Traffic Secrets*. We've literally used these books to transform our business, growing ClickFunnels to over 100,000 active members.

Most software companies are VC-backed, getting investors to dump millions of dollars to create sales and drive growth. We didn't have a penny of VC funding. We bootstrapped the entire thing ourselves. So we had to think differently and do things differently. And the way we did it was through books.

Our book funnels work like this:

When someone purchases a book, we give them something we call an "order form bump." They immediately receive the audio book and then we upsell a course of me teaching the book.

What's crazy is I might spend $20 or so on Facebook, Google, Instagram, or YouTube to sell the book. But then through the funnel, I make $40-50 for every person who buys. Because of that, I can literally spend unlimited amounts to sell the next book, so more people can hear my message. From there, I am able to introduce them to my software. That's the power of books for your marketing and your business!

*Get a free gift from ClickFunnels when you visit*
*TheShiftBookBonus.com*

## THE BUSY BOOM: HOW TO GENERATE MASSIVE LEADS AND SALES IN FIVE MINUTES OR LESS

Have you ever said, "I have so much time, I just don't know what to do with it all"? Nope, no way. Every entrepreneur is strapped for time, energy, and often capital. Everything we do needs to give the biggest ROI possible. You don't need time-sucking vampires to "brand" your way to success. You don't merely want the hope of results. You want *real results*.

And you want them now.

Here are some of the most successful strategies I have used that only take minutes each, and that you can use right now to multiply your ROI. Use them to generate a massive flood of leads today.

### SOCIAL MEDIA CLUSTER

Want to hack the Facebook, Instagram, and LinkedIn algorithms? I mean, who doesn't? To jump to the front of the line with posts and increased distribution (aka free advertising), you need quick engagement for your posts in the form of likes, comments, and shares.

Of course this can be hard when you are still growing your following, stuck in the chicken-and-egg quandary, but you can take control by forming a "Social Media Cluster." This is a group of people who will like, comment, and share each other's posts when they first run, flashing up a bat signal to the platform that yours is a popular post and should be shared with more people.

Assemble your group of people like you who are looking to grow their platforms. You each agree to support one another in posts. I suggest you create one group in Facebook Messenger that you each can use to notify the others when you post so you can all like, comment, and share, pushing your content to the top of the newsfeed over and over again.

## DROP A GIF

Want quick engagement on your posts? Instead of asking your followers to "comment below" (which is a no-no in social media channels), ask them to "Drop a GIF." These posts have high engagement and will prime the pump for your other posts.

Sample posts ideas:

- → *Happy Monday! Drop a GIF to share how you are feeling today!*
- → *Christmas is two weeks way! Yay or not ready yet? Drop a GIF below to share how you are feeling!*
- → *OMG. I was just on the XYZ Podcast! Can you say bucket list? Drop a GIF to join me in celebrating!*

Keep it fun, keep it light, and watch the engagement grow.

## P.S. SWAP

Do an email list swap with one to five other people where you each promote something for someone else in your P.S. Everyone participating in the proposition will increase their leads (including you) while you introduce your list to others you would recommend anyway.

For example:

*P.S. Speaking of time, want a system to multiply your time and increase your leads? Check out this free masterclass by Josh Turner: www. powerfulprofessionals.com/turnermasterclass*

## FOOTER BANNER

Are you using the space at the bottom of your emails? When we are in a big promotion, we use this valuable real estate for an image to promote what's coming up (see an example footer banner at TheShiftBookBonus.com).

## NINE-WORD EMAIL

Want to get your "on-the-fencers" to pull the trigger to work with you? Send a nine-word email that compels prospects to respond. You will be tempted to add more to it than this. Don't. Just leave it as is.

> **(Name),**
>
> Hey, are you still looking for (outcome of what you do)?
>
> **(Your Name)**

Your prospects hate open loops and will want to reply. When they do, that is a lead to follow up!

We use all five of these strategies often and they work again and again. Plan one or two to try this week and watch your leads and sales multiply.

Next, we'll dive into a quick way to generate leads with Facebook.

## THE FACEBOOK LIVE 7-DAY LAUNCH

*Sometimes, you've got to use an ironing board because that's all you've got.*

I was about to go live on Facebook while attending a conference away from home and needed something to raise my laptop screen. In enters the ironing board. Why I never thought of this before while traveling, I don't know, but it sure did work well. I got thousands of views, likes, comments, shares, and clicks. It set up success for a major sales campaign.

Okay, maybe it wasn't just the ironing board.

Here's the thing: I already loved Facebook Live because it is the most effective way to reach an audience organically (for free) other than emailing your own list. Even better than reaching only your own list though, you can also reach new people who are learning about you for the first time.

I love it even more now. New Facebook Live tools allow you to increase views and increase shares, even after the Live has ended. Plus, you can target those who watched your video with your next campaign, already curating an interested audience.

We've used these new features to create "The Facebook Live 7-Day Launch."

Here's how it works:

1. **Decide on a goal for the campaign.**

   Do you want to get leads with a new lead magnet? Drive in one-on-one sales conversations? Get people to show up for a webinar? Get that add-to-cart button to be clicked? Pick your goal for this campaign.

2. **Plan your content.**

   Now plan three different Facebook Lives' worth of content about your promotion topic. A few ideas:

   A. A tip or strategy in your topic area
      ➡ Weight-loss coach: Ways to get more water in your day to boost your metabolism
      ➡ Dating coach: Places to meet single people
      ➡ Business coach: Email subject lines that get opened
   B. Success stories of those you've worked with
   C. Answer questions about your niche that you found at Answerthepublic.com

3. **Go-Viral Facebook Lives**

   Seven days out, run your first Facebook Live using the "Go Viral" system:

   A. Open your Facebook Live with a countdown to create engagement before going on camera. This gives Facebook time to invite people to your Live. Participate in the Chat comments to create engagement before you go Live and fuel the fire of Facebook's video distribution.
   B. I use Zoom to screenshare on Facebook Live and set up a countdown page with ClickFunnels. When the countdown ends, stop sharing your screen and turn your video on, teasing your viewers that you are going to give away a prize, but they have to stay on to win. This will create engagement and keep people on-air until the end.

C.  Next, share your pre-planned content, continually asking questions of your audience and giving feedback.

D.  Share what your prize is going to be and let them know they have to guess correctly to win. An easy one to do is write down a number on a piece of paper, actually writing it while on the air. Tell your viewers they will have an extra chance to win if they also share the video right now to their network.

E.  While they are making their guesses, answer any questions that came in or give one more piece of content, teasing the future promotion that is coming up.

F.  Award the prize to the winner and close out the Facebook Live.

## MULTIPLY YOUR RESULTS AND REAP YOUR REWARDS

Repeat this process twice more in seven days, offering different content each time but on the same topic. Then, it's time to get your viewers to take action. Create an audience of them to target your ad toward. Next, we'll go beyond social networks, into your dream prospect list. No magic wand required!

## HOW TO LAND YOUR "DREAM 100" CLIENTS WITH $5/DAY AD SPEND

Throwing spaghetti against the wall to see what sticks (aka trying a bunch of things to see what works) is how most entrepreneurs would describe the way they currently market. Thankfully there is a better way.

Let me ask you a question. Did you ever get an email, DM, or text message from someone you admire who wanted to work with you, and you almost couldn't believe your eyes? A dream come true? Perhaps you grabbed your phone and alerted loved ones to share the news before you even hit reply because you were so freaking psyched and still couldn't believe it.

But yes. It indeed happened. Best of all, you didn't even have to chase this prospect. They came to you.

Well, what if you could get that type of lead every single day? By going after your "Dream 100," a targeted list of 100 dream prospects, you can focus on just those you really want, and quickly reach them without wasting time or money on others.

## ⏻ POWER EXERCISE

1. Craft a list of people you really want to work with—from clients to JV partners, even media outlets you'd like to have cover you.

2. Fill in the email address, phone number, and mailing address for anyone whom you already have contact information.

3. For the remaining contacts, connect with your Dream 100 on LinkedIn using the following request:

   **(Name)**, *I've always admired your work at* **(insert company)** *and I would love to connect here.*

   By going after your Dream 100 on social media, you can focus on just those you really want, and quickly reach them without wasting time or money on others.

4. Once you are connected, go to their LinkedIn profile, and click on "Contact Info." Pull any listed information into your spreadsheet.

5. For anyone not listed on LinkedIn or still missing contact information, use Hunter.io to supplement. You can pull up to 50 contacts a month at no charge from this site simply by typing in the company name.

6. Once your list is complete, upload it to Facebook as a Custom Audience.

7. Start a series of Facebook Lives giving useful tips and strategies to your audience. This sets you up as an authority and expert, which is exactly what you'd like your Dream 100 to see.

8. Boost your Facebook Lives to your Dream 100 List for $5 per day in ad spend.

9. Download your Facebook Lives and upload them to LinkedIn so your new connections see your content there as well.

10. After four weeks of appearing in the newsfeed of your Dream 100 list, it's time to advertise to them with a call to action, driving them into your sales funnel. Simply target your Dream 100 list with this new batch of ads.

11. For your top-of-the-list dream clients, follow up one-on-one during the campaign sequence to see if there is interest in taking the next step with a conversation.

12. After you cycle through one group of 100, repeat the same sequence for the next.

Focusing on your Dream 100 gives you the power to land your top dream prospects as clients, garner desired media coverage, and even score deals with JV partners that you've previously only dreamed about.

Next up are a few bonus strategies to multiply your ROI.

## BONUS HOLIDAY PROMOTIONS

Great marketing can find any reason to make things time-sensitive. One of the most obvious to leverage is when my BFF (pumpkin spice) appears, when the lights start twinkling and turkeys get nervous. This is my favorite time of year. Every day has a bit of a sense of wonder and magic. It's why I start burning Winter Forrest WoodWick candles in August. (Judge as you will, but if the wick-crinkle in summer is wrong, I don't want to be right.)

When it comes to business, holidays can also mean a huge sales surge. They give a time to create excitement and time-sensitive calls to action. Plan ahead and multiply your sales.

Here are some promotional ideas for seasons at the end of the year:

### HALLOWEEN

No tricks, all treats. Hold a week of promotions in different candy themes to give treats to your list, like:

➡ A different content strategy or daily tip with a promotion in the P.S.
➡ Bonuses with a purchase

- ➡ Added services when a contract is signed
- ➡ Gift with a prospect meeting
- ➡ "You've Been Booed." Along the lines of the kids' game of leaving treats behind, gift your list, customers, clients, or patients with a free workshop, training, or template. Include a promotion in the P.S.

## THANKSGIVING

- ➡ **Thanksgiving Eve.** In honor of this night of celebration, hold a promotion to celebrate the exciting opportunity for your list.
- ➡ **Black Friday.** When your list is in the shopping spirit, run a promotion that gifts them a credit, offers a special gift with purchase, or adds a bonus. Last year we ran a flash sale for the holiday with some of our courses and it was our biggest non-webinar sales day of the year.
- ➡ **Cyber Monday.** This is the biggest online shopping day of the year. Jump in the game with a promotion to drive quick action to your list.
- ➡ **Thankful for These Things.** Put together a resource list of your favorite products, programs, and services using partner and affiliate links.

## CHRISTMAS

- ➡ **12 Days of Christmas.** Create 12 days of flash sales to your list.
- ➡ **Charity Promotion.** Gift a percentage of sales for a day during the holidays to your charity of choice. Kramer Photography did this, gifting a free portrait with a donation to the Susan B. Komen organization. They raised over $15,000 for the charity and drove over $63,000 worth of clients into the center.
- ➡ **Best of Party.** Run your webinars, promotions, workshops, or top content from the year. Plan these ahead of time and take the week off while sales still come in. For the week between Christmas and New Year's last year, we replayed a different webinar each day as a gift to our list.

Leverage these moments and more holidays to develop reasons to buy all year long.

Next up, we'll dive into how to break through the clutter of what your prospect is hearing.

## ⏻ POWER EXERCISE

We've tested including GIFs in our emails and it increases click-through and email response rate. But to amp up our engagement, we tried creating our own GIF, and it worked!

**How to do it:** Using the Boomerang app (download first to your phone), take an image of a video clip. I like to use a moment in my webinar where I had hand motions. Then, insert it in your email and link the GIF to your landing page or promotion.

Try this for your next email series and test the results!

## THE MONEY METRICS ON SOCIAL

When it comes to getting lots of attention online, the answer is obvious. Of course, you go outside during the perfect light with amazingly flipped hair, a happy/curious/smart/inquisitive smile on, head tilted back and laughing while the sun just starts to set. Your image shows how fit, smart, kind, and funny you are. Or even better, it shows you just the way you are.

You then craft the most amazing caption ever that is the perfect mix of witty, inspiring, and thought provoking. Those that read it will instantly become a better person just for seeing your content. Seriously? No. Be real. Be you.

*You aren't looking for a gazillion double taps.*
*Because, my friend, you can't take that to the bank.*
*You are looking for clients.*

Not surprisingly, this next technique works. Every time.

While the "gurus" would like you to think you can "filter-image" your way to success, we know better. But when a post goes "viral" it attracts real prospects who become your customers, clients, and patients. While posting to get clients isn't as simple as "finding the right light outside," it doesn't have to be complicated.

Follow these steps to create a viral buzz the next time you post.

## 1. FOCUS ON THE OUTCOME

When it comes to using your social media content to drive in prospect appointments and sales, you've got to first start with the end in mind by answering this question:

*What problem will you solve for your prospect if they ultimately purchase your thing?*

For instance, if someone purchases our 6-Figure Course Blueprint program they will be able to sell their expertise one-to-many and automate sales 24/7 to a course through an evergreen webinar.

For Power Tribe and Inner Circle Member Howard Globus, an MSP IT firm owner, if one of his clients uses his services, they won't have to worry about losing productivity if their systems go down or missing a call when someone is out of the office or losing much worse because of a security break from an innocent "download this file" request.

For Power Tribe and Inner Circle Member Violet White, a health coach, her clients will be able to lose weight, improve their health, and keep it off while not feeling like they are starving themselves or being deprived.

These are "outcomes." Find yours and then move to step two.

## 2. PICK FOUR SUB-TOPICS THAT LEAD TO THE SALE

When it comes to content, choose topics that create interest, make a case, or answer objections about your topic.

For instance, when it comes to launching a digital course, some topics I could talk about are:

- ➡ How big your list should be before you launch a course
- ➡ How to automate a webinar to sell a course

- → Pricing options for courses
- → What makes a good bonus for selling your course
- → My favorite webinar technology
- → Tech 101 for course creation

Brainstorm four sub-topics about your subject matter.

## 3. GO LIVE
Each week go live with your sub-topic for that week, offering tips and strategies about your topic area.

## 4. AFTER THE LIVE
After you go live, get the most out of your content:

- → Add captions to the Facebook Live.
- → Email your list a link to the Facebook Live video. (Optional, embed the Facebook Live on your own website.)
- → Create a post on LinkedIn and Twitter, driving back to your Facebook Live.

## 5. REACHING YOUR IDEAL PROSPECTS
With social proof of viewers to your video, boost your video to your Dream 100 audience. Repeat the same strategy each week for the month.

## 6. FLIP VIEWERS INTO BUYERS
Create an audience out of those who watched your video and retarget them with an ad to join your webinar, or schedule a sales appointment, or whatever your offer may be.

Your content only shows to people who have already shown interest in your topic and see you as an expert. Then when they opt-in/sign up for a prospect call, you are already perceived as the authority, and they are much more likely to buy from you. Way better than simply clicking "Like."

Next, we'll dive into a way to simplify how you post so you don't have to feel tied to the computer or phone.

## POWER STRATEGY: FACEBOOK'S CREATOR STUDIO

If you'd like to take some time off over the summer or next holiday season, preschedule your content using Facebook's Creator Studio/Publishing Tools. This will allow you to schedule posts to both Facebook and Instagram at different times and add links to your Facebook posts and hashtags to your Instagram Posts.

Here's how:

1. Go to Creator Studio/Publishing Tools.
2. Choose Post.
3. Create and schedule for Facebook, leaving out any links.
4. Schedule for Instagram.
5. Edit the Facebook post to add in the link if you want to include one.

(See what this looks like at TheShiftBookBonus.com.)

That's it! Your posting will continue without you being live—the best free assistant Facebook has to offer!

Continuing on with this chapter are more strategies you can use to multiply your lead flow.

## POWER STRATEGY: AUDIENCE AVALANCHE IDEAS

Want to quickly grow your online audience? Make sure you are using all of these spaces where you can get leads:

1. Create a lead magnet free gift. This can be a simple downloadable checklist, workbook, or mini course.
2. Put the link everywhere you can, including:
   ➡ Cover photo of all social media
   ➡ The "About Us" on all social media
   ➡ Your bio link on Instagram
   ➡ Your email signature line

3. Find organizations that you can sponsor to give away your gift. Brainstorm groups that have similar audiences to yours but are not competitors and ask if you can sponsor an upcoming event or purchase a sponsored email. This strategy has allowed us to quickly grow our audience and coaching groups and was well worth the investment.

4. Pre-schedule posts to go out at least once per week showing a link to your free gift. It is easy to let time slip away and miss a chance to grow your list. Ensure that never happens again by scheduling your posts ahead of time using Facebook's Creator Studio scheduling tool.

5. Grow your following consistently on Facebook so that your audience is fresh and engaged, sending a siren out to Facebook that your content should be shared with others.

**Remember: Your audience is waiting.**

As we round out this chapter, you have more strategies you can use to reach your target market.

## POWER STRATEGY: YOU DON'T NEED LUCK WHEN YOU FOLLOW THIS SOCIAL SELLING STRATEGY

Here's a quick way to generate content so you're not constantly hustling to think of new ideas:

1. Go to Answerthepublic.com and find the top questions asked in your niche.

2. Create a post on Facebook or Instagram answering one of those questions. (Use the Word Swag app to create a great image with the question, then answer it in the post.)

   ➡ Share a link to that post on your other social platforms to drive engagement and traffic.

   ➡ Screenshot the post and engagement and share it on LinkedIn with commentary and elaboration on the content.

Ta da! You've just turned one question and answer into a lot of content that features you as the authority and expert. How's that for a shift in thinking?

## POWER STRATEGY: QUOTE YOURSELF

Who has two thumbs, is really smart, has a cute smile and should be quoted more often? You, of course. In fact, one of the quickest ways to build authority and gain brand equity is to be quoted by others in the

things that you say, aka "the gems you drop."

You can make this happen more quickly if you start quoting yourself and creating quote posts. You can use Canva or my favorite design app, Word Swag.

Go into your existing content, your lives, your blogs, a quoted interview, or proposals, and pull out thought gems to use as quote posts. Then simply design and post them.

While it is weird to talk about oneself in third person (so Kim should never do that) it is not weird to quote yourself in your content. You can build your brand around that. If you don't tell others how to quote you and what messaging your clients and super fans should share, they won't know what to do. But if you start to tell them the "how" and give them the message to share, they will. And the more you are quoted, the more brand equity and authority you gain.

An easy-peasy yet super effective strategy.

## POWER STRATEGY: SHIFT YOUR MESSAGING

The secret to effective marketing? Make your thing about *them*, not you.

I was recently ordering Starbucks via Uber Eats and fell in love with the tipping page. They make you the hero for tipping a lot by tying a value-based kudo to each level of tipping.

I've always done this when writing copy for donations or fundraisers. Don't make it about the donation. Rather, make it about the impact the donor will have. The same is true for business—don't buy from me, make your goals come true instead.

## POWER STRATEGY: GROW YOUR LIST WITH YOUR DMS

Imagine a way to grow your list that requires no funnel, no landing page, and no ads. Yup, simply add the term "DM me" to your social posts and you can.

Here's how:

**Line one:** Ask a question.
**Line two:** Tease a solution.
**Line three:** Tell them to DM you a word.

Our coaching members recently tried this and are getting results that are paying off.

Try it today!

Now that you've filled your anti-hustle toolbox with ideas that will help you make the shift from overworked to worry-free business owner, let's meet someone who makes his business out of leveraging the leads you'll get from those efforts—Ryan Levesque.

## ⏻ LEVERAGING YOUR LEADS

The number-one thing my target market wants is more leads. No one know leads better than **Ryan Levesque**. He sat down with me to share not only how you can leverage more leads for less than you thought possible but leads that are high converting and super easy to get.

Ryan is the ultimate authority in this revolutionary way to get more leads. He's the five-time Inc. 5,000 CEO and creator of *The ASK Method*, the best-selling marketing book of the year. His work has been featured in *The Wall Street Journal, Harvard Business Review, Forbes, Entrepreneur,* and *NBC News.* He's also the co-founder of bucket.io, which is the world's leading quiz funnel software technology with over 30 million end users worldwide.

**Kim:** *Let's talk all things quizzes! Ryan, why the heck do quizzes work to generate qualified leads for our business?*

**Ryan:** It's important to set the stage that we're not talking about those online quizzes like "What Disney princess is your dog?" type. We've all seen them before. Maybe some of us have actually taken them. Those are fun, but they're not going to convert clicks into clients. What we're really talking about is when someone lands on your website, and instead of seeing a traditional lead magnet (like "Download my free ebook"), you ask a series of questions, like a doctor trying to diagnose and recommend the best next step for someone. These questions feel to your prospect like you are having a one-on-one conversation with them, except your website is having that conversation with a thousand people a day, 365 days a year on autopilot.

There are all sorts of benefits to doing this, but cheap leads, higher conversion, hard data, better selling, and better serving are just the beginning.

**Kim:** *I've heard from my coaching clients who leverage quizzes that these leads are much less expensive. Why do you think that is?*

**Ryan:** There are a couple things at play. At the highest level, you're tapping into the psychology of self-discovery. You're inviting someone to discover something about themselves.

Pay attention to your own physiology as you hear these two different situations. In scenario one, you're scrolling Facebook. You see a post that says, "Click the link below to get my ebook." In scenario two it says, "Click the link below to find out your unique results." It's so much more enticing. What happens is the latter encourages people to actually start the process.

Another thing at play that is responsible for driving down cost-per-lead is that a well-designed quiz funnel adds value for your prospect. You're giving people instant results and answers of what to do about it. This content is very shareable. Your prospects will share a well-designed quiz funnel, sending it viral, and all that free referral traffic drives down your cost to advertise.

Another force at play is that whatever platform you post your quiz to has a goal to improve their users' experience. Quizzes are something that people comment about and share their results. They'll say, "Oh, I took this quiz, and my result was..." Then someone else takes the quiz and shares because of seeing their friend's action. People hit the like or love button, then share. It gets all this great engagement. That sends a message to the platform to expand your organic reach. They'll show your content to more people simply because it's getting such great engagement.

In turn, this drives down your CPM (cost per thousand impressions) if you are running paid advertising. The platform makes it less expensive for you to advertise, allowing you to get more people to take your quiz because you're tapping into the power of micro-commitments where they answer little baby-step questions. Instead of paying people to give you all their information, you're getting people to share it for free. The social media platforms shift onto your side, working with you instead of against you. The net effect is a cost-per-lead decrease anywhere from 30-90 percent when you switch over to using a quiz funnel.

**Kim:** *Then do you put the next step on the thank-you page? Or do you recommend following up via email?*

**Ryan:** When you can customize your copy and messaging based on someone's quiz answers, you get the power of cheap leads with dramatically higher conversion. Give people their results right then and there. Then get clear on what the next step is that you want people to take. Is it to buy your product? Book a call with you? Watch your webinar or workshop? Join your challenge or your free group? Invite people to take action immediately after they get their quiz results. We often see our clients double or triple their sales conversion rate on the back end of the quiz. The reason is intuitive.

**Kim:** *It brings to mind Robert Cialdini's book,* Influence. *He talks about the concept of tribe mentality and how we have this aching need to be part of a tribe for safety. It's in our DNA. A quiz prompts curiosity:* How do I fit in? How do I relate to others? *Once you uncover for them which tribe they fit into, you can show social proof from specific people who match up with that tribe. Now we're not just catering our sales offer, but also the social proof that speaks to who you are and what you believe in.*

**Ryan:** Something I've taught for years called "testimonial mismatch" goes like this. Imagine for a minute that we think all testimonials present good social proof. In reality, the wrong social proof—even positive social proof—can actually negatively affect your conversion, *unselling* people on buying from you.

Here's an extreme example just to illustrate the magic. You and your sweetheart are heading to a tropical, romantic getaway. You want to do something super special, so you go to TripAdvisor and look at hotels in the destination. You find one that's rated 4.8 stars out of 5. Instantly you think, *This is gonna be perfect!* Then you look at the first review. It says, "OMG, most amazing hotel in the world. My buddies and I partied all night long. The beer was super cheap, and they let us blast the music. Best party of our lives. 5 out of 5."

Well, that review was amazingly positive, but what is your first reaction?

**Kim:** *Ick.*

**Ryan:** You are not going to stay there, right? That is not a romantic getaway place. That's an example of a testimonial mismatch. The hotel had great social proof, but showed it to the wrong person, actually unselling them on booking.

A quiz funnel allows you to connect the right client experience with the right client testimonials, based on someone who is just like them, so it feels like they're looking into a mirror.

**Kim:** *That's so powerful. It really lets us know about our market. Maybe there's something we didn't recognize until we see that 90 percent of people answer a certain way. Then you can refine your* *marketing to go after those people more easily, without spending so much time or resources on folks who finish the quiz with other results.*

*Can you help readers imagine how this can work in their industry by giving a few examples from different niches?*

**Ryan:** We've helped businesses of all different shapes and sizes, selling either physical or digital products through low-ticket and high-ticket offers. Our team has helped build quiz funnels in 63 different countries in 47 different languages. We've seen this transcend culture, price point, and industry.

Morgan Gist MacDonald is a coach who helps people publish a book. She created a quiz: *What publishing path is right for you?* If you've published a book before, you know you have so many choices, right? Do you self-publish or traditionally publish? Do you offer an ebook? Do you do paperback or hardcover? Audiobook? If so, do you narrate it yourself? What platforms do you post on? There are *so many* decisions. So Morgan created this assessment to help people identify which one's right for them. Now in the back of this assessment, she invites people to book a call with her where she will review their quiz results with them. Then she sells a $15-30k coaching package through that process.

For someone who sells physical products, I think of Snack Nation, a company that sells a curated box of snacks that they mail out based on your food preferences, allergies, dietary needs, and the number of people in your home or office. They use a quiz funnel to ask the right questions so they can recommend the right package for you. They were able to triple their business, growing to over $24 million a year on the back of a quiz funnel. In a split test comparing their quiz conversions versus the traditional eCommerce model, they found the quiz more than tripled their average order value. They were also able to cut their sales cycle in half while increasing people's reorder frequency... all on the back of the quiz.

Why is this true? Because these businesses are able to put the right message, the right content, and the right offer in front of the right person at the right time instead of just trying to guess.

If you sell courses online, I think of Neil Gordon and his quiz: *What's your public speaker type?* He brings in six figures a month teaching people how to become a better public speaker, selling online training courses on the back of his quiz. Whether you are selling a super high-ticket coaching consulting package, digital product, online course, or a physical product like a box of snacks, the quiz funnel generates cheaper leads with dramatically stronger conversion rates.

**Kim:** *Speaking, snacks, and serving my market are three of my favorite things! How can someone begin to develop an idea about what their quiz should look like?*

**Ryan:** First, they need clarity on what next step they want people to take after completing the quiz. One of the biggest mistakes I see is people who build a quiz akin to a staircase that leads to nowhere. Instead, figure out what next step the prospect should take. Is it booking a call with you? Buying your book? Watching your workshop or webinar. Once you've decided, you can start brainstorming process for figuring out what type of quiz makes the most sense for your business.

There are three types of quizzes that work better than anything else: Type, Killer, and Score.

A *Type* quiz helps people identify what type of something is right for them, or what type they are. An example is "What's your public speaker type?" or "What type of business is right for you?"

A *Killer* quiz helps people identify the biggest mistake they are making in an area of their life that you help them with in your business. I think of Charlie Wallace, who helps people make faster progress learning the guitar progress. His quiz asks people, "What mistake are you making when it comes to learning to play the guitar?"

A *Score* quiz helps evaluate where someone is along a success path or journey. Are they Level 1, 2, or 3? Once you can determine the gap between where they are right now and where they want to be, then you can help them find the best next step to take to close that gap—which is presumably to buy your product or service.

Consider which of those three quiz types will make the most

sense for your business. Is there one that fits better than the rest? If they all might fit, just pick one.

**Kim:** *I love that. I always tell people, "You're going to be certainly uncertain. The only way to become truly certain is by taking action."*

*Get a special gift from Ryan (and a bunch of goodies from me) at TheShiftBookBonus.com.*

# 07

# A POWERFUL PROFESSIONAL

## Power Thinking vs. Common Thinking

**THERE IS AN** image in my head of ocean waves crashing at the beach while I dig a hole in the sand. I'm trying to dig as fast as I can to make a hole deep enough to withstand the waves. That is how I imagine my mission to reach as many people as possible while fighting the messaging of others out there telling you to "hustle and grind."

I want to combat this dangerous teaching. When you're constantly focused on the hustle and grind, you're missing out on life: your own, and that of your loved ones. In this chapter I want to open your eyes to a new way of approaching business that allows you to tap into what most people don't even realize they're missing about the opportunities in front of them. It's time to notice the difference between everyday Common Thinking and the far stronger Power Thinking that will make your clients, customers, or patients feel as if you are reading their minds to provide amazing experiences they never even dreamed were possible. This is the thinking that makes you an anti-hustle-and-grind Powerful Professional.

One day in early 2022, I walked into a medical complex and came across this sign that was the ultimate in dumb Common Thinking. It said:

*STOP—DO NOT ENTER*
*Do not enter asking for directions.*
*If you are looking for a doctor's office, Do not enter, the directory*
*is beside the elevator.*
*You MUST have a mask on to enter this office.*
*This office is open by appointment only.*
*Do not enter unless you have an appointment.*

I mean, this office has a flow of people coming in all day long who are looking for help. Instead of seeing a way to provide great customer service and even generate future business, they saw it as a hassle to be avoided, even at the cost of confusing their current client base and putting future business at risk.

My guess is a lazy employee convinced the boss it was a good idea to put up a sign that would keep people from accidentally wandering into the wrong place. But it backfired horribly. What if instead, they had put up a sign saying, "This is a private medical office. To protect the privacy of our patients, please do not enter unless you have an appointment. For a building directory, scan this code. If you would like to book a future appointment with this office, text xyz," or something like that?

Their very Common Thinking was: "I don't want to be bothered."

Power Thinking goes more like this: "How can we use this moment to exceed expectations and set ourselves apart in the marketplace?"

Which kind of thinking do you lean toward?

## LEVERAGE YOUR POWER THINKING

The good news is, not only is it quite easy to exceed the terrible customer service your competitors are presently offering, but you can also leverage Power Thinking in your content creation. Let's walk through how to easily create content that will set you apart in the marketplace.

# ⏻ POWER EXERCISE

Start by making a list of 5-10 things you don't fancy about your competitors, but that you either already do differently or would like to find a better way.

Here's mine to get you thinking:

**Ten Things I Don't Like that Other "Gurus" Do**

1. Teaching that you must "hustle and grind" to be successful. Forget about your friends, family, and health. Work all the time.
2. Strategies focused on "Be everywhere all of the time."
3. Teach things they don't do themselves.
4. Leave out steps so things look "super easy."
5. Only share the "big numbers" and not the numbers that led to that big number.
6. Keep members hostage in contracts they didn't understand when they signed up.
7. Have a great sales game but weak content and teaching.
8. Forget to give the promised "bonuses."
9. The "final deadline" is never final. There is always some lame "internet glitch" excuse to re-open a promotion.
10. Each item sold is just a way to sell again.

Now it's your turn to make your list:

1. _____

2. _____

3. _____

4. _____

5. _____

6. _____

7. _____

8. _____

9. _____

10. _____

Once you make your list, the next step is to chart out what you do differently (or want to do differently in the future) as opposed to what you don't like.

For example, using my list from above:

| COMPETITORS' COMMON THINKING | OUR POWER THINKING |
|---|---|
| Teaching that you must "hustle and grind" to be successful. Forget about your friends, family, and health. | You can have an Empire Business and Lifestyle Business at the same time. |
| Strategies focused on "Be everywhere all of the time." | We only teach strategies that have been proven for at least 90 days. |
| Teach things they don't do themselves. | We only teach strategies we use in our own business. |
| Leave out steps so things look "super easy." | Full transparency on the step-by-step so that the strategies we teach can be accomplished. |
| Only share the "big numbers," not the numbers that led to that big number. | Tell the real story behind the numbers. |
| Keep members hostage in contracts they didn't understand when they signed up. | No contracts. We earn the memberships of our clients each month. |
| Have a great sales game but weak content and teaching. | Focus on serving our members. |
| Forget to give the promised "bonuses." | Track all bonuses and ensure they are always delivered. |
| The "final deadline" is never final. There is always some lame "internet glitch" excuse to re-open a promotion. | Stay with the integrity of a deadline, always. |
| Each item sold is just a way to sell again. | Serve hard so you can sell easy. |

Now, add a column for your Power Thinking philosophy:

| YOUR POWER THINKING |
| --- |
| 1. |
| 2. |
| 3. |
| 4. |
| 5. |
| 6. |
| 7. |
| 8. |
| 9. |
| 10. |

Next, draft a story that results from your Power Thinking:

| COMPETITORS' COMMON THINKING | OUR POWER THINKING | STORY |
| --- | --- | --- |
| Teaching that you must "hustle and grind" to be successful. Forget about your friends, family, and health. | You can have an Empire Business and Lifestyle Business at the same time. | Making it to the kid's softball game. |
| Strategies focused on "Be everywhere all of the time." | We only teach strategies that have been proven for at least 90 days. | Membership Outrageous Offer... the real aftermath. |
| Teach things they don't do themselves. | We only teach strategies we use in our own business. | Specifically do things to test so our members can use them. |
| Leave out steps so things look "super easy." | Full transparency on the step-by-step so that the strategies we teach can be accomplished. | The non-talking spray and the hot-mess express spray tan. |

| COMPETITORS' COMMON THINKING | OUR POWER THINKING | STORY |
|---|---|---|
| Only share the "big numbers," not the numbers that led to that big number. | Tell the real story behind the numbers. | First-launch airplane story. |
| Keep members hostage in contracts they didn't understand when they signed up. | No contracts. We earn the memberships of our clients each month. | Timeshare situation. |
| Have a great sales game but weak content and teaching. | Focus on serving our members. | Focus on serving over selling. |
| Forget to give the promised "bonuses." | Track all bonuses and ensure they are always delivered. | Basecamp system. |
| The "final deadline" is never final. There is always some lame "internet glitch" excuse to re-open a promotion. | Stay with the integrity of a deadline, always. | Countdown strategy. |
| Each item sold is just a way to sell again. | Serve hard so you can sell easy. | The "You Make a Difference" segment of staff meeting. |

Once I draft the first story, other ideas come to mind. Keep this chart handy to add more. (Download a copy you can fill in and print out at TheShiftBookBonus.com.)

Next, create content to support your ideas that can be batched out. Here are a few strategies to get the most out of your Power Thinking:

1. Schedule time to record a video walking through each of your Power Thinking philosophies vs. the Common Thinking. (Savvy strategy: Schedule them using Stream Yard so they can publish like a live video but still be pre-recorded. These videos can broadcast live on YouTube, LinkedIn, Facebook, and Twitter at the same time.)
2. Create an Instagram Reel with each of these concepts.
3. Write an email for each and schedule them.

4. Create a post for each that has an image of you and long-form content.
5. Keep these concepts in front of you when you are a guest on someone else's podcast to mention them and set yourself apart from competitors.
6. Record a podcast episode about each.
7. Every week in your Clubhouse room, start with a Common Thinking vs. Power Thinking concept.

Pulling from this content allows you to show up authentically without having to figure out "how do I show up authentically." It just is. Leverage this strategy as you reach your market.

## POWER THINKING RULES TO LIVE BY

"I love being underpaid and overworked and not appreciated for it," said no consultant or coach, ever. Yet why do so many do it? I'll tell you.

They are scared that if they don't, they will lose a client, not get another one, and end up being a failure who is talked about by that high school jerk-face who still influences their decisions even though no one has seen them since the five-year reunion.

Just stop that nonsense for a hot minute.

How could you get **more** clients who actually pay you what you are worth **and** still have a life you love?

By getting your Power Thinking on.

Power Thinking is different from Common Thinking. Because of this, it produces different results!

Here are a few of my favorite Power Thinking rules that I live by:

1. Want to pick my brain? Pick your payment method first. My expertise took a long time to gather. It is expensive, and worth every penny. No, "taking me for coffee or lunch or dinner" is not enough payment. But maybe we could talk about a private jet to the Bahamas...

2. You can't be a jerk-face to my team, even if you are nice to me. You will kindly be invited to find another coach.

3. I am A-OK knowing that I may not be your cup of tea. Turn that cup over so I won't waste time pouring into you. I prefer to spend my time filling up those who are thirsty for my flavor of No-BS, ROI-based coaching.

4. You can message me on the evenings and weekends, my sweet clients, but a response is not coming back to you until regular working hours. We are clear on that from the start, so expectations are always met.

5. I am only going to work with you if I would love to hang out with you. So if you are my client, I don't just like working with you. I really like you.

Start with one or two of your Power Thinking rules to live by, and when you make a decision, stay strong. Not only will you like your everyday more, but you will attract clients who value your non-negotiables and want to work with you because of it.

Next, let's dive into how to build your celebrity, authority, and expert status as you do just that.

# 08

# STANDING OUT IN A SEA OF SAMENESS

## How to Create Your Own Unfair Competitive Advantage

**LITTLE KNOWN FACT...** Before I saw the light and became a direct-response social media strategist and business coach, I was a celebrity event planner and public relations specialist. Yup, I worked with the fancy people to promote their fancy things.

On the positive side, I had access to a lot of top-shelf champagne, rides on big boats, and swag bags to swoon over. On the negative side, my clients were prone to tantrums, unrealistic requests (no, the New York Yankees cannot come to your birthday party tomorrow) and tended to treat my team like last week's issue of *People*.

Eventually, I would change careers, but it gave some good stories to dig into, like this one:

A fabulous former client who is still a friend to this day, Stephen Asprinio—"The Villain" of *Top Chef* on Bravo—hired me to help plan the opening party of his restaurant in West Palm Beach, FL. The restaurant was all things Stephen: non-apologetically complicated, upscale, and delicious. And so would be his opening night party.

When I presented the event plan and décor scheme, he stopped me abruptly. "The red carpet cannot be red. Of course, it must be purple. This specific purple, to be exact." Stephen pulled out a fabric swatch that matched the signature color of his restaurant. (Like I said, he was unapologetically complicated.)

So I hightailed it out of there, with a week to scramble and find a purple carpet for opening night. Not an easy feat more than a decade ago. But you know your girl came through, and that purple carpet was in place before the shiny dresses and shoes made their way on it for photos.

You know what? Stephen was right to ask for the precise purple carpet. He was clear on how he should be represented and the details that mattered in making it so. People took pictures all night long standing on his signature purple carpet, promoting his signature brand.

To this day, Stephen is paid six figures and more per restaurant project to consult on their brand and design aesthetic.

So that brings me to you...

What are your non-negotiables for your brand? Do you insist on consistency of messaging and representation? Do you have a signature look? Signature phrase? Signature offering?

Picking your "thing" can help you to stand out in a sea of sameness and rise above the clutter, making you the "attractive character" others want to be around. That's what we're talking about in this chapter. Are you ready to have your purple carpet moment?

## GETTING YOUR CELEBRITY ON

Every year billions of dollars are spent on celebrity endorsements. People will buy whatever celebrities eat, drink, wear, and drive. They want to know what celebrities do, where they shop, where they live, and where they do business. Tap into celebrity, and you have access to the most powerful marketing force available.

Why? Because fame creates authority.

You can become a celebrity yourself. It's actually pretty easy. If you do business on a local level, it's even relatively inexpensive to become a local celebrity. If you do business nationally but in a niche market, it's also relatively inexpensive.

You don't have to wait for the *Today Show* to call or for Oprah to ask to interview you. You can create your own celebrity. Here's how:

1. Get a professional headshot. This is the place to amp up your game and go beyond the selfie. Celebrities have good photos, and so should you. To find an affordable photographer in your area, check out a site like Thumbtack.com. You can post the job there, and photographers will apply to take your photo, giving an estimate up front. You can usually get a good headshot for less than a night of table service at a hot spot in town.

   You can also search *#(insert name of town)photographer* on Instagram to find photographers and see examples of their work.

2. Create your cover photo. Using free templates at Canva.com, create your cover photo using your professional headshot and an offer with your USP, your unique selling proposition. I switch mine if I'm holding an event or promotion, or just working on building my email list.

3. Feature your content in your posts. If you're sharing other people's content more than 10 percent of the time, *stop*. Your social media pages are *your media*. Use them for positioning your own message. This is your opportunity to shine and set yourself up as an expert in your industry, so feature your content, and develop your own images and posts.

   If you don't know where to start, begin by creating a list of 25 questions your prospects tend to ask when you meet with them, and start by answering those. That will give you almost a full month of posts.

   Or use a site like Quora.com. There you can identify the most popular questions people are asking in your industry. Make a list and start your posts by answering those.

4. Have good people. Pull in your "team" to help. (After all, celebrities have people, don't they?) There are great resources

on sites like HireMyMom.com, Fancy Hands, and Textbroker. com to get your posts written, images designed, and to schedule them for you.

Ready to walk the red carpet to prospecting success? Then make sure all of your networks reflect your brand. And don't be afraid to get help where you need it.

And speaking of help, here are 100 content ideas for your social media content creation.

## ⏻ CONTENT CREATION IDEAS

- Create a daily, weekly, or monthly series
- Run a contest or giveaway
- Host an "Ask me anything"
- Run a social media takeover
- Share some related content from others
- Repurpose your own content
- Host a challenge
- Create a how-to or tutorial
- Celebrate "National Whatever Day!" (Different quirky holidays)
- Make a meme
- Make a GIF
- Give customers the spotlight
- Do a "This or That" poll
- Go behind the scenes
- Share a milestone
- Share a reading list
- Tap into a trending topic
- Share a playlist
- Show your product in a surprising situation
- Make a slow-mo video
- Share some wisdom
- Showcase user-generated content
- Share secrets or hacks
- Post a recipe
- Ask your followers for advice
- Fill in the blank (Create a post for your audience to answer such as "Today I am grateful for____")
- Congratulate someone for an achievement
- Introduce your team members
- Do a charity drive
- Tease a product drop or upcoming release
- Brag about your reviews
- Remind people who you are, and how you got started
- Share a personal Story
- Share a joke (graphic or text)
- Share a quote (graphic or text)
- Share your favorite book
- Ask for recommendations (books, TV, apps, music, something related to your biz)
- Tell people to sign up for your email list
- Give away a coupon
- Host a sale
- Go LIVE (Live videos perform amazingly well)
- Share a blog post you wrote
- Give your audience a gift
- Share any press or PR features you have

- Host a 1-Day Only flash sale
- Post a case study
- Answer FAQ's
- Share a WIN or SUCCESS
- Share a LOSS or a FAILURE
- Host an interview with a guest
- Post a link to your own interview
- Post something seasonal or highlight a holiday
- Thank your fans!
- Post Motivational Monday
- Post a Tuesday Tip
- Post a Wednesday Wisdom
- Post a Throwback Thursday
- Post a Flashback Friday
- Share a short video clip (yours or one you like)
- Share a podcast episode you love
- Share a YouTube video you love
- Post some interesting stats or data about your industry
- Share a Tweet you like
- Share your other social profiles to connect on
- Share your favorite resources (apps, websites, blogs)
- Share your morning routine
- Post about events you're hosting or going to attend
- Post where you'll be speaking or where you're making appearances
- Share an unknown feature about your products or services
- Share your contact info
- Post about a trip you've taken
- Post about something on your bucket list
- Ask your audience how they found you
- Make a countdown
- Show that you or your brand cares about the environment, society, local community, or animals
- Show how your product is manufactured
- News (hare current world events that are important to you)
- Share infographics
- Share links to free resources
- Image scrambles (or blurred). You'll have your audience scratching their heads in no time when you post image scrambles—where an image is scrambled up or zoomed in, so your audience has to guess what it is.
- Host a Twitter Chat
- Share a survey
- Ask user opinions about something
- Re-post an old post
- Ask fans to share photos with your product
- Host a live conversation with a leader or prominent figure in your industry
- Ask the mood of the fans
- "Do you remember" posts
- Share a series of images—a gallery depicting your recent office party, product launch, or anything else
- Hold a debate
- Ask for predictions
- Share-if. Ask your fans to "Share" the post if they match whatever the post is. Like, "share this post if you love pineapples on your pizza"
- Ask a "truth or myth" question
- Post affiliates
- Post a reaction video
- Share your weekly schedule
- Share your daily, monthly, weekly goals
- Share your favorite coffee or other beverage
- Share your meals for the day
- Share "what I'm currently binge watching"

## USING THE POWER OF SOCIAL INFLUENCE TO GET YOUR PROSPECTS TO SAY "YES"

Imagine you are in a small town, away on business, and are starting to get hungry. You notice two restaurants in the town square. One has two cars in the parking lot—you are guessing a server and the cook's car—and the other has 20. Which one are you going to choose?

Your brain will most likely pick the safer option, of course. No matter what they've got on special this evening, you are going with the one that has the cars in the lot.

Why do we do this? Social behaviorist Robert Cialdini calls this human behavior "informational social influence." It is the concept that people copy the actions of others in certain situations out of a desire for safety. It's why we'll buy something online that has more reviews than something else that doesn't. It's why we ask, "What are you wearing?" to our friends before going to a new event. It is also why most wait for others to rise before they stand up at church or at a concert or sporting event.

We protect ourselves by choosing something others have done before us.

But it's more than an awakening of why you pick your restaurants or even cheer for the team you do. It is about how to leverage growth inside your company using this phenomenon. That's the key to getting your prospects to say "yes."

So, how do you leverage that growth? Getting to "yes" starts with you and is all about how you can shift your company's story from history to influence. Use these tips to generate more social proof, trust, and persuasion in your marketing:

1. **Tell stories of your customers in your marketing copy.** When you showcase what you do/sell/offer, share stories of your own customers as examples of how what you sell delivers on what you promise. Get as specific as possible because each time you add actual numbers and specific details, it provides social proof.

2. **Interview clients in your content.** Feature your past and current customers in your content regularly. We run an interview each month with one of our coaching clients, giving

them the spotlight and showcasing the type of people who work with us. This creates interest in what we do and helps our prospects see themselves working with us. It also helps our current clients build their own celebrity and authority for what they are doing well.

3. **Awards.** Showcase your best success stories and give your prospects something to shoot for and a clear path to success. We have used awards successfully in our coaching program, featuring students when they launch a course and hit five figures in one hour, then six figures, seven and beyond. Not only is it really flipping fun to celebrate our members, but it creates convincing social proof.

4. **Grow your social following.** If you visit a person's social media page and they've got only 43 followers, it doesn't give a whole lot of confidence that they are the ultimate authority on what you are hiring them for. The same is true for your business. People want to work with the "in-demand" choice for their niche. Having a large following and social proof increases persuasion for a prospect to take the next step with you. Having more followers propels post engagement by creating instant trust for new people who see your post in your newsfeed. We've been teaching how to quickly get followers for a long time, and it is amazing to see the improvement in online success with our students who make the change.

Whether you leverage multiple social influence strategies or just start with one, there is incredible power in highlighting those who have chosen to do business with you before others do.

Try social influence as the ultimate leverage point in increased leads and sales.

For a bonus training on how to quickly get thousands of followers for your business page, and to see an example ad from the "10X Your Followers Challenge," visit TheShiftBookBonus.com.

# 09

# POWERFUL PROFITS

## Turning Your Prospects into Sales on Autopilot with the Winning Webinar Blueprint

**WHEN I FIRST** got that nudge to take myself out of the everyday of my business and free up time to be more present, I was listening to Russell Brunson's podcast *Book Expert Secrets*. We were living in New Jersey at the time and I remember the exact spot along my walk, the boat I saw in the water, and the sound the pebbles made below my feet.

Russell explained that to finally grow, he had discovered that he couldn't keep launching different products, programs, and services. Instead, he had worked on perfecting one webinar that he presented over and over again.

When I heard this, I felt a bolt of lightning. My face got hot, my pulse sped up, and I started to jog home while I left a frantic voicemail for my marketing director. I said, "We've got it. I am going to do a webinar and I am not going to stop until we get it right."

And that's exactly what we did. I created one webinar and presented it 119 times, testing something different each time, in essence creating a Winning Webinar. This model came from testing the strategies many different gurus suggested and combining it with sales and persuasion techniques I've developed over time. In this chapter, I'll walk you through the blueprint you need to set up your Winning Webinar so you capture the "yes" as organically as possible. Then, in the next chapter, I'll show you how to build that Winning Webinar.

## THE FOUR WINNING WEBINAR BELIEFS

Once you craft your Winning Webinar, there's no more doing it over and over again. For myself and my coaching clients, if a live webinar converts at least 10 percent of attendees into a sale, then we automate that webinar so the video sells while we do other things, like write this book. Or play with the kids. Or wonder how the *Real Housewives of Miami* keep their hair always looking like they just left the salon. (Seriously, the humidity in Miami is no joke.)

Now, the purpose of the webinar may shock you.

While the Winning Webinar's purpose is to give great value, it is not to teach any "how-tos." In fact, if you start teaching in a webinar, you've lost the sale. You will have overwhelmed the prospect and done a downright disservice to them.

If you are convinced you have to teach in your webinar, then I challenge you to examine whether or not you care more about the prospect liking you than you do about serving them through getting them to take the next action with you.

**The purpose of a webinar is to show the prospect what is available to them on the other side of saying "yes" to the opportunity you present at the end with your offer.**

What I realized was that if an individual believes these four things to be true before I make the offer to work together, he or she is most likely to say "yes."

Those four beliefs are:

1. The solution you have is the solution to their problems and what they woke up praying/wishing/hoping for.

2. You are the right person to show them how, or to sell them the product, or to do the service to accomplish their goals.
3. They are not broken, but the thing they tried before was, and they can have success with your program.
4. Bonus belief: Others will be super impressed and excited when they do it. There will be visible proof and an elevation of status when the person engages with your program, buys your product, or uses your service.

Instilling these four beliefs is the primary objective of the messaging that allowed us to quickly scale from 32 clients to more than 11,000 in just one year.

## THE WINNING WEBINAR BLUEPRINT

There's not much that I brag about, but this webinar formula works like a charm. In fact, I was at a dinner with our Inner Circle members the evening before writing this chapter and our member Jana Danielson shared that she's generated over $100,000 in the last three months using this template to sell a fitness program.

Inner Circle member Laura Lea Sparks brought in $34,790 in monthly recurring revenue selling to attorneys.

Inner Circle Elite member Todd Tramonte used it to generate more than $100,000 in five minutes selling to realtors.

The blueprint works if you use it. Here are the five components:

1. **Engagement:** There are certain things you will do during the webinar to create engagement and compliance. This ensures your prospect is paying attention, keeping your presentation front of screen, and getting accustomed to following your directions, which will be very important when it comes time to click on your offer.
2. **Social Proof:** To feel safe enough to move forward with your offer, your prospect wants to see that others have joined the webinar with them and that others have taken the offer and

had success before they did. We strategically use social proof throughout the presentation, both in engaging attendees and in showing examples of what worked in the past.

3. **The Big Idea:** An effective webinar focuses on the "Big Idea," the outcome the prospect is craving, not the work to get there. The Winning Webinar continually brings the prospect back to what they want so they can see clearly that your offer is the obvious solution they want.

4. **Time Sensitive Call to Action:** No matter how remarkable your offer is, if there isn't a reason for your prospect to act now, they won't act at all. And even though it might seem totally cheeseball, having a fast-action bonus will drive in more sales because there has to be a reason great enough for your prospect to choose to overcome their fear. Give them a good thing that will come to them if they take action now.

5. **Framework:** Apple has the iPhone. Starbucks has the Venti. You will have a framework. This is a proprietary breakdown of how someone can have success with you and the thing you do. Make it simple, memorable, and desirable by using an acronym to build out a 4-step (or less) framework.

Here are some examples of Winning Webinar topics our clients have developed from this simple framework:

### What is Scale F.A.S.T. Formula Live?

Simply put, Scale F.A.S.T. Formula Live is a virtual 3-day, high-energy and high-impact event where you'll discover the fastest way to scale your business, such as:

F: Find your perfect target market (who).
A: Acquire A.C.E. status to bring your buyers to you.
S: Scale your sales with a Client Generation Machine.
T: Turn your clients into an unpaid sales force.

### L.E.A.D. Magnet Book System

- L: Laser-Focused Goal
- E: Expert Interviews
- A: Acquire Best-Selling Status
- D: Dominate Sales

### The S.M.A.R.T. Estate Plan

5 Time-Sensitive Changes to Make Before Your Child Goes Away to College

- S: Set goals for your children and yourselves.
- M: Make sure you can access information and provide assistance when needed.
- A: Absolve burdens from your spouse and children.
- R: Relieve your family from chaos or confusion in your absence.
- T: Take care of your family in their greatest time of need with good planning/detailed guidance.

### The Keep Them Happy Leadership Formula System and Toolkit

How to lead your team to more productivity, positivity, and performance excellence by leading with metrics, not magic.

- L: Leverage the power of "I can" by empowering your team to leverage your vision in their decision-making.
- E: Engage employees in the "Disney way," empowering them to operate as a unified front to best serve your clients, customers, or patients.
- A: Acquire "Trusted Leader and Advisor" status, becoming the sought-after expert beyond your team to your peers, multiplying your Authority within those you manage.
- D: Double your team's productivity and performance by tapping into the science of the mind of your employees.

**The G.R.O.W. Your Authority Plan Program**

The Wellness Practitioner's Guide to Becoming the Market Leader of Your Niche, Attract Higher Paying Clients, and Multiply Your Revenue

G: Get clear on who you want to reach and why.

R: Reach your market with one key magnetic message.

O: Own your space, building authority, celebrity, and expert status in our niche.

W: Welcome in new opportunities that come with your new place in the market.

Once you create your framework, it's time to make the magic happen with your webinar. In the next chapter, you'll discover the Winning Webinar formula to do exactly that.

# THE POWERFUL PRESENTATION

## The Winning Webinar

**AS I MENTIONED** in the previous chapter, back when I was scaling the business and looking to get out of selling one-to-one, I created a webinar to sell our services. And as you read in the previous chapter, I did that webinar 119 times.

For reals. Without fail, one hour a week, I did the webinar:

- ➡ from Disney with the family.
- ➡ in the middle of a meeting.
- ➡ from Paris on vacation.

No matter where I was, I stopped and gave my webinar. And I was often asked why.

It is because that was my most profitable hour of the week. Sometimes I made $3,500 and other days it was $74,298. But it was always worth it, because I tested what worked and what didn't until I perfected the model.

Then I used the best recording in an automated webinar that generated $2.74 million in revenue for us in less than one year.

Still till this day, we use this same Winning Webinar Blueprint, and our coaching clients do, too.

And now, it's all yours!

Plus, if you want a PDF of the slides, you can get yours at TheShiftBookBonus.com.

On the next several pages, you'll find the slides as well as scripting and insider tips for building and hosting your own Winning Webinar. Let's dive in! An example script is listed with each slide, where applicable.

**SLIDE 1**

*Welcome! Thrilled to have you on here today.*

*Before we get started, let me know, can you hear me? Comment in the chat if you can hear me.*

[Read a few names.]

*Okay, cool thanks. Now, really important, I want to make sure you can see my slides. I was on here for a while last week and I went for 10 minutes with none of my slides showing, and it was really embarrassing. So let me know in the chat if you can see my slides. Okay, great, [name] can see them, [name] can see them. Awesome.*

*Well, welcome everyone! Before we get started, let's make sure we give our full attention because I'm going to give this my everything and want to make sure you do, too. So put your phone on silent. In fact, that is what I am going to do now* [put phone on silent], *and you should, too. Now close out of Skype, Instagram, and Facebook. I know there are fun things on there but nothing on Facebook is going to make you a millionaire right now* [or say whatever outcome you are teaching] *but what you are about to discover when you give this your full attention, just might. Grab a pen and paper and get ready to take good notes because you will discover* [repeat outcome].

**SLIDE 2**

*So I can better serve you, I have to get to know a bit about you. Put into the Q&A* [Ask a question here. It could be something as simple as where you are from.]

*And I want you to know where the Q&A is. Throughout our time I am going to ask a bunch of questions. Sometimes I will tell you to put your answer in the Q&A, and other times I am just asking questions and I want you to respond in there. Also, I love to see your a-ha moments, so when you hear something that you really like or is a big takeaway for you, go ahead and put that a-ha into the Q&A.*

*So starting right now, let's find out* [Repeat question and read a few answers].

# POWER STRATEGY:
# BRING PERSONALITY INTO YOUR
# ENGAGEMENT STRATEGY

While sitting poolside on vacation perusing the drink menu, a webinar strategy came to my mind. (I mean, a girl has got to do what a girl has to do.) Two of our coaching clients are also Power Coaches, Lou and Tami Santini, and one of their programs teaches travel advisors how to become destination wedding planners. They open their webinar by asking, "What's your favorite tropical drink?"

It's a fun spin on an engagement question to ask at the start of your webinar. Maybe asking your attendees if they are more of a pina colada or a margarita person wouldn't fit your niche but consider asking some type of curiosity-building question to generate engagement.

It's important to do because it:

➡ fosters engagement early on, which creates a commitment to stay for the whole workshop.

➡ generates social proof when you read answers aloud, so attendees feel they aren't alone.

➡ gets your attendees accustomed to using the chat box, which will be important when the link for the offer is placed there.

➡ wastes a bit of time, which is necessary because most people show up late for webinars.

All of that in one little question.

The reason why our webinar framework works so well is because it is built on a blueprint that has been perfected over time and performs every single time we use it.

Try adding in little moments of personality, surprise, and delight to increase engagement and connection with your attendees.

**SLIDE 3**

*This is for you if...*

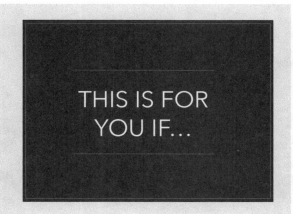

**SLIDE 4**

[Read slide]

**SLIDE 5**

[Read slide]

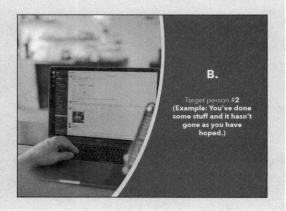

## SLIDE 6

[Read slide]

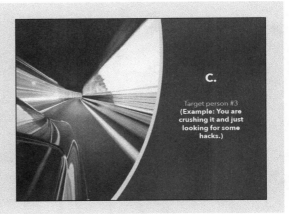

## SLIDE 7

*Which are you: A, B, or C?* [Repeat options by reading a few names for each of the options.]

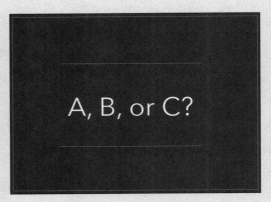

## SLIDE 8

Remember the framework we set up earlier? Here's where your framework goes.

## SLIDE 9

Read the slide and elaborate on each reason why it isn't their fault. Those reasons should not be about them personally but should be about external reasons.

## SLIDE 10

*But that all ends today. Because today you will discover* [say the outcome].

## SLIDE 11

*Let's play for a second and imagine you can wave a magic wand.*

## SLIDE 12

*And* [Say outcome 1]. [Example outcome: You got to work with the exact clients you wanted.]

## SLIDE 13

*And* [Say outcome 2]. [Example outcome: You had people begging to work with you.]

## SLIDE 14

*And* [Say outcome 3]. [Example: And your sales multiplied over and over again.]

**SLIDE 15**

> You see,
> I get it.

**SLIDE 16**

Use a photo that represents what your life was like before you made a change.

*Back in* [time frame], *I* [talk about what life was like at that time].

Slide 1 with picture of your before story

**SLIDE 17**

Choose another photo that represents what your life was like before you made the change.

*I even* [Give example of it being not what you envisioned, etc.]

Slide 2 with picture of your before story

## SLIDE 18

Now it's time for your epiphany story part 2.

*But then* [Get really specific about a time that things didn't go well. Give as much detail as possible, but no more than 4 min]

**Something Had To Change**
Conflict that forced you to seek a resolution

## SLIDE 19

Now tell your epiphany story part 3.

**The Breakthrough**
Discovery/Resolution

## SLIDE 20

*So you are probably thinking, sure, that all sounds good, but why are you teaching this,* [your name]? *Why am I teaching this? Well* [give your reason].

**Why Am I Teaching This?**
One big reason.

**SLIDE 21**

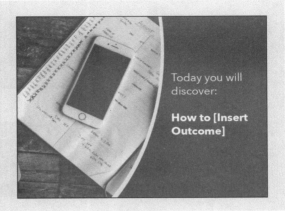

**SLIDE 22**

*But before we move on, let's address an elephant in the room.* [Share an objection and why it isn't valid.]

[Example: "I need to be a great writer to have a best-selling book."]

**SLIDE 23**

[Say your outcome statement.] *Do you want this?*

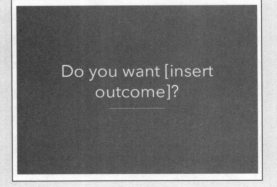

## SLIDE 24

*A study by Harvard Business Review showed we are 5 times more likely to achieve goals when we write them down. Now is your chance to 5X your results by typing "I'm in" into the Q&A.*

## SLIDE 25

This is where your framework goes. Keep it simple and tightly worded for this slide.

## SLIDE 26

*How?*

**SLIDE 27**

*This is how. Let's go over each part of the formula step by step.*

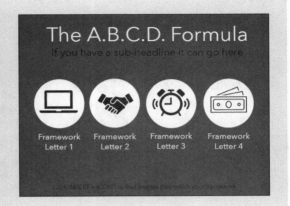

**SLIDE 28**

**SLIDE 29**

Talk about the outcome of Framework Letter 1.

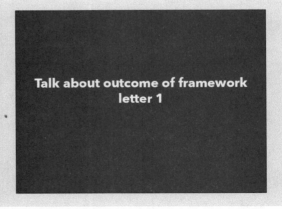

**SLIDE 30**

Give an example of
Framework Letter 1.

Repeat these three
slides for each
letter/step of your
framework.

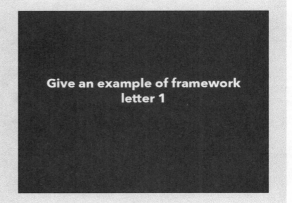

Let's see what this looks like in practice. Starting below, I show you my own use of this framework for the first letter in my formula (then you can repeat/replicate for the other letters in your own framework). Oh—and you'll notice that there are no script notes for these as they are specific to what I am providing. You'll create your own script following the suggestions I've mentioned earlier.

**FRAMEWORK
SLIDE 1**

**FRAMEWORK
SLIDE 2**

**FRAMEWORK
SLIDE 3**

**FRAMEWORK
SLIDE 4**

**FRAMEWORK
SLIDE 5**

10 people on a
webinar =
1 sale

**FRAMEWORK
SLIDE 6**

Just 10 people on a webinar
and just 1 sale each week...

**$48,000**

**FRAMEWORK
SLIDE 7**

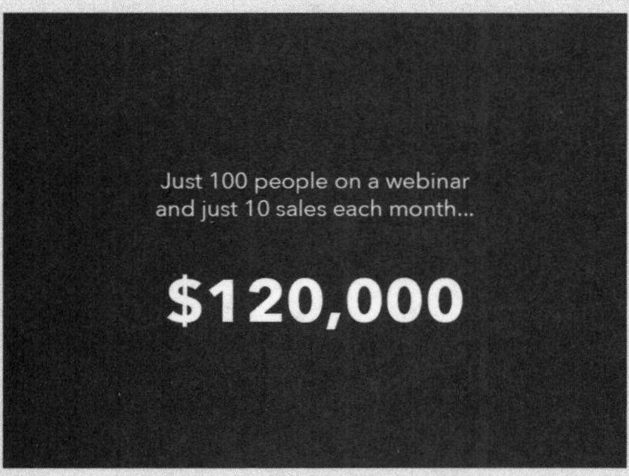

Just 100 people on a webinar
and just 10 sales each month...

**$120,000**

**FRAMEWORK
SLIDE 8**

Just 100 people on a webinar
and just 10 sales each week...

**$480,000**

**FRAMEWORK
SLIDE 9**

Focused on one book and one
webinar.

**$480,000**

**FRAMEWORK
SLIDE 10**

It's just that simple.

**$480,000**

**FRAMEWORK SLIDE 11**

You can quickly launch a course and multiply your **Impact and income.**

**FRAMEWORK SLIDE 12**

Just like...

**FRAMEWORK SLIDE 13**

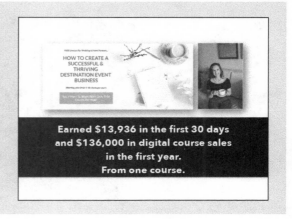

Earned $13,936 in the first 30 days and $136,000 in digital course sales in the first year. From one course.

That's an example of how I do the first letter in my formula. You can repeat the steps here for each letter of your own framework. When you're done, it's time to bring it home.

**SLIDE 31**

*Do you want [outcome]? If so, type "yes!" in the Q&A right now.*

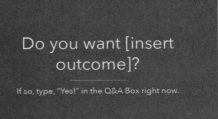

**SLIDE 32**

*Just like...*

### SLIDE 33

Give example of
someone who has
achieved outcome
either in your program
or in pop culture.

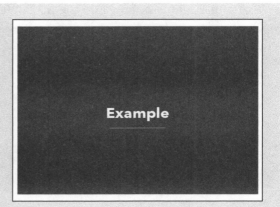

### SLIDE 34

Give example of
someone else who
has achieved outcome
either in your program
or in pop culture.

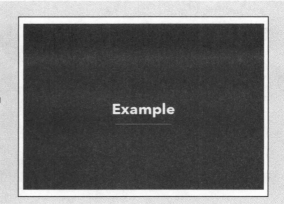

### SLIDE 35

Give third example
of someone who has
achieved outcome
either in your program
or in pop culture.

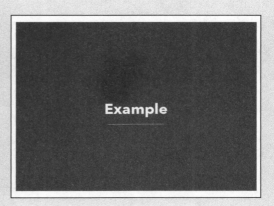

## SLIDE 36

*I hope you get this one thing* [the big idea they need in order to believe in order to buy].

(I hope you get this one thing)

The Big Idea They Need To Believe In Order To Buy

## SLIDE 37

*You might be wondering...*

You Might Be Wondering...

## SLIDE 38

*How can I* [outcome]?

How can I [outcome]?

**SLIDE 39**

*You have the slow way, through trial and error and you can never get back the money or the time you spent away from your family that was wasted trying to get results. Obviously, you are here, so you can get results. With your permission, I'd love to show you how you can get results you can see in your bank account really, really quickly.*

**SLIDE 40**

*Here's how. It's the* [name of your program, which you are mentioning for the first time].

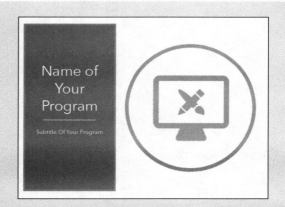

**SLIDE 41**

*But before I get all excited and tell you how you can [outcome], I've got to tell you who this isn't for. If you'd rather make excuses than make things happen, this program isn't for you. Because this program was created to [what it will do].*

**SLIDE 42**

Read program name and subtitle again. This repetition is intentional.

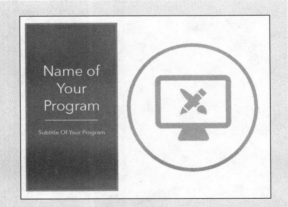

### SLIDE 43

*Let's look at* [name of program] *and walk through what to expect.*

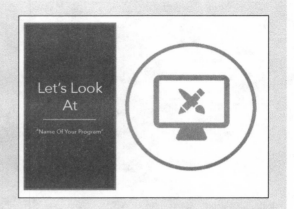

### SLIDE 44

Give name and outcome of Module 1.

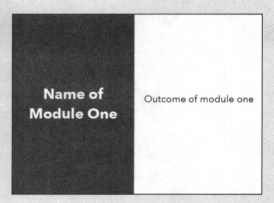

### SLIDE 45

Give name and outcome of Module 2.

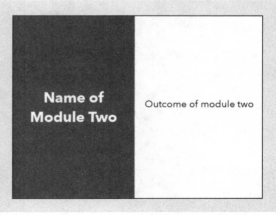

**SLIDE 46**

Give name and
outcome of Module 3.

Name of Module Three — Outcome of module three

**SLIDE 47**

Give name and
outcome of Module 4.

Name of Module Four — Outcome of module four

**SLIDE 48**

Repeat the outcome
once again.

Outcome of the Program Repeated

### SLIDE 49

*Your program will include* [components].

Program Components

- Immediate access to course portal
- Live Q&A
- All sessions recorded and transcribed
- All slides, handouts and checklists

### SLIDE 50

*Plus you get my personal help.* [Share details.]

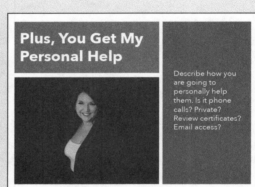

Plus, You Get My Personal Help

Describe how you are going to personally help them. Is it phone calls? Private? Review certificates? Email access?

### SLIDE 51

*You also get a special bonus:* [name of bonus and outcome of bonus].

Title of Bonus
Value $XXX

•Outcome

## SLIDE 52

*And, in addition, you get to stack another bonus:* [name of additional bonus and outcome of bonus].

## SLIDE 53

Name all of the items and the total value.

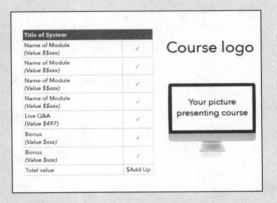

*But before I tell you about the special opportunity just for you, right now, I have a question for you. What would this be worth to you if you could [outcome]? What would that be worth to you? If one week from now you could [outcome] what would that be worth to you? If one month from now [outcome], what would that be worth to you? If you finished your year [outcome], what would that be worth to you?*

**SLIDE 55**

**YOU GET EVERYTHING**

$V~~al~~ue

$W~~eb~~ Price

For only 3 x $Multi pay price

Or Save X with a One-time investment

*Now, the value of the program is \_\_\_\_.*

*But we are going to do better than that. Even better than our web price of [amount] to [outcome] for only one payment of [amount] and two more investments of 30 days apart of [amount].*

*Or save [X dollars] with a one-time investment.*

*But before I give you the URL, I've got a warning and that is, you must go there quickly. The thing is, in just a minute, I'm going to give you a fast-action bonus. Now this fast-action bonus will be worth [outcome/value] in just the next 30 days alone.*

*And you might be thinking, "Huh, that seems like a lot of pressure she's putting on me right now. Why would she do that?"*

*Let me tell you... if you think I'm putting extra pressure on you just to get you to take action right now, you are right. That's exactly what I'm doing. Because I know the difference this program has made in my students' lives and the lives of our families, and I am going to do everything in my power to get you to take action right now. Even if that means giving you a fast-action bonus that is worth more than the price of the program itself. Okay, ready to click?*

**SLIDE 56**

*Go right now to the chat bubble and see the new link in there [name of link]. Click on it. It will bring up a new browser so you can quickly fill out the form and hit submit. Or you can open up a new browser right now and type in [URL].*

**SLIDE 57**

*And while you do, let's go over our 14-day, money-back guarantee. You have double what other programs give you and we are giving you 14 full days to go through the program and if you do the work and it doesn't work for you, you get a full refund.*

## SLIDE 58

*Imagine...*

> **IMAGINE...**
>
> **Course URL**

## SLIDE 59

*It's 1 week from now and [outcome].*
*It's 1 month from now and [outcome].*
*It's 1 year from now and [outcome].*

## SLIDE 60

*Ready for that fast-action bonus that is worth five or six times the price of this program again and again [or whatever your outcome is]?*

> FAST ACTION BONUS

**SLIDE 61**

Here is what you'll get for acting fast: [Name of fast-action bonus and outcome of bonus.]

NOTE: I know we have a lot of bonuses to keep track of, but remember that this one is special, as it's just for those who act quickly.

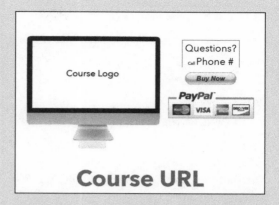

So open up a new browser right now and go to [URL].

Or give us a call at [number].

We take PayPal, Mastercard, Visa, and American Express.

You are going to get [name the programs].

To get the on-air pricing, the on-air bonuses, and the fast-action bonuses as well, open up a new browser and type in [URL].

If you have questions, put them in the Q&A, and while you do, I will go over a few questions I often get. [Give those questions and answers.]

[Go over your "you are probably thinking" belief statements, then answer other questions.]

[Then read some new customers' names.]

[Answer other questions.]

Thank you for joining me and allowing me to share with you the system that has changed my students' lives and my life. But you know what? The biggest thing that happened was [life transformation].

And I want this same exact thing for you. You get all of the tools and templates... everything that you need. All you have to do is be willing to make the investment in yourself. Hey, my life isn't going to change when you sign up. I am not going to go out to dinner any more often. I am not going to go on vacation more. The person whose life changes when you take action is you.

And that's the Winning Webinar blueprint. Use this formula to leverage your framework and sell one-to-many with your audience.

Conduct your webinar at least three times live. You will feel more confident each subsequent time, and your presentation will benefit. Then, as long as the webinar converted at least 10 percent of attendees into a sale, make the webinar evergreen, using a recording to give your webinar on autopilot instead of live. We use a software called Easy Webinar and it produces sales for us on autopilot. That's the ultimate shift—getting leads generated while we are doing other things. As we close out this chapter, we'll move into ways to uplevel your webinar ROI once you get started.

## POWER STRATEGY: ADD LIVE CHAT INTO YOUR AUTOMATED WEBINAR

Already running an evergreen webinar and want to multiply your sales? Try adding in live chat.

As we are ever-testing how to multiply the ROI of what we do, we have tested many ideas on what helps to multiply sales of our evergreen webinar. The one that had the greatest impact was adding live chat to the automated webinar.

The Easy Webinar software comes with a Q&A box that automatically delivers these chat message to your email account. We found a setting to swap this built-in option to forward to your chat service instead. (We use ClickDesk.)

Since adding live chat, our sales percentages have doubled. Try adding chat to yours and see what it does to your numbers!

## UP-LEVEL STRATEGIES FOR AN EFFECTIVE WEBINAR

When it comes to producing an effective webinar, I do not believe in "winging it."

Instead, I follow the framework, slides, and script because that is what works. Not to do that would be akin to a heart surgeon saying, "You know, I am so tired of using the scalpel. I am going to try a plastic fork this time just to mix it up."

Bad idea.

The template works.

There are however some up-level strategies to utilize once you get the template working for you.

1. **10X that energy.** Your energy is diminished a lot by the camera. Why? I don't know. And if I did, I probably would have gotten a bigger scholarship to college than I did. I do know that it's true, so you need to be you, but with more "oomph."

2. **Smile often.** Some people call it resting-think face (or worse) but whatever it is, I have it. And it doesn't look good on camera. Before my wedding day to the Tall One, I actually trained myself to smile for the entire day so I wouldn't inadvertently be caught with an unattractive expression. It worked and I love my photos from that magical day. I've used that same skill on webinars to smile for the entire time, because if I can't be excited about what I have to say, who can?

3. **Demonstrate the behavior you want given back to you.** At the start, as you explain that attendees should turn off their phone

and grab a pen and paper, demonstrate yourself doing the same thing so that the camera can see. People are much more likely to do what you say if they can see you doing it, too. Let your viewer see "behind the scenes." During my webinar, there are a few moments when I "break the wall." This means I tell the viewer what is going on, just like those moments in *The Office* when Jim would talk straight to the TV camera. It creates the feeling of "we're in this together" and builds trust. For example:

When I read a testimonial by Kevin O'Leary, I say to the viewer first, "Here's where I read a testimonial from a famous person I have worked with in a way to build trust with you because you have a better chance of knowing who he is than you do who I am."

When I share that there is a fast-action bonus, I say, "Now, the value of the program is ___, but we are going to do better than that. Even better than our web price of (outcome) for only one payment of (amount) and two more investments of 30 days apart of (amount). Or save (x) with a one-time investment. But before I give you the URL, I've got a warning and that is, you must go there quickly. The thing is, in just a minute, I'm going to give you a fast-action bonus. Now this fast-action bonus will be worth (outcome) in just the next 30 days alone. You might be thinking, *Huh, that seems like a lot of pressure she's putting on me right now. Why would she do that?*

"Let me tell you...if you think I'm putting extra pressure on you just to get you to take action right now, you're right. That is exactly what I'm doing. Because I know the difference this program has made in our students' lives and the lives of our families, and I am going to do everything in my power to get you to take action right now. Even if that means giving you a fast-action bonus that is worth more than the price of the program itself. Okay, ready to click?"

During the Q&A, I share, "If it sounds like I'm trying hard to enroll you,

I am. That's because I owe it to you, and I hope you'll do the same thing for your students.

4. **Lead off Q&A with some questions.** When you start the Q&A, ask for them to put questions in the chat, but share that you will start with a few you always get and then answer the questions you would want to have answered.
5. **Chat your way to the sale.** When the webinar is over and the Q&A is done, don't close down the webinar. Instead, be available to answer questions privately in chat. You will always have prospects who aren't comfortable asking questions publicly but will buy if their questions are answered. Make sure to give them a chance to do that.

Most of all, the more you conduct your webinar, the better results you'll get. Eventually, your Winning Webinar will work for you while you are doing something else!

In the next chapter you'll discover what you are actually going to sell on your Winning Webinar.

# 11

# THE POWERFUL PROFITABLE BUSINESS SECRET

## A Course

**I KNEW I** had stumbled onto something amazing when I finally found my gateway to an anti-hustle working life. The first person I called when I found out was my work wife, Kelly LeMay. I shared what I had just learned and told her we should bring all of our clients together and start a new service for them. We agreed to host a breakfast and a lunch using a trade we had left over with one of our partners (I was really good at bartering work-for-food back then) and started inviting clients to come.

**What was this big discovery?**

This was 2011 and I had uncovered the world of Facebook paid and organic lead generation and was about to pivot from a PR and Branding Agency to a direct-response lead generation firm.

As I stood in front of our clients at these planned meals, I showed them what was possible and pitched this new service offering. One after another signed up. In fact, we had a 100-percent upgrade in our client services. It was an easy sell because they saw me as the "expert" presenting to them something new that could grow their business.

Let's be real: I wasn't some guru or certified ads person. My ads knowledge had come from attending one conference on word-of-mouth marketing, but that was enough to boost me into "expert" status. Because an expert doesn't need to know everything. The expert just needs to know enough to be a few steps ahead of those they serve.

Our client base grew, and their results continued to crush industry norms. Word-of-mouth spread and I began to be asked to coach individual business owners on how to use Facebook to grow their business.

I loved coaching. I loved seeing my coaching clients succeed and how it changed their lives. What I didn't love was how much time it took. Each client required an hour of my time each week, plus time answering emails and texts. I was working around the clock and was starting to burn out.

It hit me, though, that I was answering the same questions over and over again and giving the same advice.

*What if I could find a way to put all of them together in a group and teach them at once? And generate more revenue so we could invest in advertising.*

It was around this same time that I bought a course from a business mentor I had been following, all about becoming a paid speaker. With my growing reputation of being a social media lead-generation specialist, I was starting to be asked to speak at events and I wanted to figure out how to navigate it. But even after buying this course, I was less interested in the content and more interested in how the creator put together a course to teach many at one time.

I paid $7,500 using the payment plan option and paid for another program. I took doing this next course—and breaking down the course creation process—seriously. Like, nerd on fire, notebook, Post-Its, and highlighters in hand seriously. After studying not just this course, but every speech or event I could attend or get my hands on, within 30 days I had launched my first online course.

## MY LAUNCH

Not really getting the whole one-to-many thing, the course I launched was $5,000 and included 30 days of one-on-one coaching for Facebook Ads. Even though this was still going to require my time, it was way better than the $100/hour I had been getting from one-on-one coaching clients.

Now, at the time, I had a small list of less than 1,000 people, but I launched anyway. We were blown away. Fifteen people bought, generating $75,000. O.M. Goodness. And while it was a bit nuts for a month of coaching these new folks, only a few wanted to start right away. The rest trickled in over time.

**And it kept going.**

Every few months we would run this offer again and drive in new coaching clients, many of whom ended up becoming ongoing agency accounts. I also quickly added a course-only option that didn't include any hands-on help for $997 and that started selling quickly as well.

In fact, our first livecast of selling that program became my first six-figure launch, generating **$113,000 in sales in just four hours.**

I knew this was a game changer.

**I could finally serve many while not having to work around the clock.**

The growing education component to our business is eventually what led to my decision to sell our agency. I knew I could coach many more people if we no longer offered one-on-one services.

It was around this time that Josh Turner of LinkedSelling made an offer to buy my company and was the perfect partner to sell to because he already ran a similar model for LinkedIn clients. Josh still uses the 30-day Rocket Launch sales model to this day.

Since selling our agency, we've been able to scale our coaching company from $150,000 in sales to multiple seven figures and landing the #475 spot on the Inc. 5000. I went from being able to work with a max of 30 businesses in our agency to serving more than 11,000 amazing clients and members last year alone.

It's been an amazing journey and even though I have been in business forever, it feels like I am just starting. I am thankful I decided to scale, serve more, and get paid to do what I love. How about you? Interested in exploring how to turn what you do into an automated funnel that can serve many?

## POWER STRATEGY: PAUSE BEFORE ANSWERING

Yep, we all do it.

When someone asks a question of whether or not they should buy our thing, we are likely to jump back with a retort of the reasons why they should.

But we are always better served in first asking, "Why did you ask?"

Case in point: A message came in about our course on creating courses and the prospect asked, "Is coaching support included in the course?"

Now, there is support included but instead of answering that, I first responded, "I love that question, and I can't wait to answer it, but so I am sure to give you the answer you are looking for, would you mind sharing why you are asking?"

His response, "Well, I want to create a course, but I don't have time to do ongoing coaching for my students."

Because I asked, I found out what was important to him and was able to respond with, "Great question! You can simply do a Q&A call once a month and answer any questions that come in then."

Which is exactly what he needed to know, but that's not the answer I would have given with his first question.

When you are asked something, pause, refrain from answering and instead say, "I love that question, and I can't wait to answer it, but so I am sure to give you the answer you are looking for, would you mind sharing why you are asking?" first.

Often that is the exact question you need to ask to get the answer you are looking for.

# THREE WAYS TO LAUNCH YOUR COURSE

"One Size Fits All." My 4'11" self knows this statement is not true when it comes to clothing. It also isn't true when it comes to launching a course. From having coached hundreds of entrepreneurs through their first course launch, I have identified three types of launches that multiply time and passive income for their creators.

## SUMMIT LAUNCH

You may not like this one. This is only for you if you want instant social proof, list building, and a quick way to generate sales. (See what I did there?)

Summit Launches are fantastic ways to grow your list before your main course launch and/or to create a boost in your list creation. A lot of my students just getting into list building have used these, but it isn't just for them. I use a Summit Launch about once a year and did so most recently with the publishing of my last book, *The No B.S. Guide to Direct Response Social Media Marketing.*

The way that it works is, you pick one big idea or topic and invite speakers on to your Summit to be interviewed about their area of expertise. Those individuals share the Summit with their lists, and you offer recordings of the Summit as an option to purchase.

When Inner Circle member Suzi Seddon did this to kick off her coaching business, she ran one about Facebook Groups. She grew her list by 634 new people and generated 135 sales of her recordings. Power Up member Tanya Auger did the same recently to kick off her health coaching business and she was able to generate net profit while growing her list.

## LIST LAUNCH

This type of launch is for you if you have a list already of 250 people or more. You start by inviting just these folks onto your webinar to enroll in your course. This audience is most likely to convert into a sale, and it provides a no-cost way to launch. Once you sell to this audience, you will create the course live with them each week with your modules and then have a course you can sell over and over again.

Power Up member Judy Hoberman recently launched her S.K.I.R.T. Selling System to her internal list and generated over five figures in sales with just getting started. She's recording the course now with these early buyers and will be able to sell the course ongoing moving forward.

## EXTERNAL LAUNCH

These are the launches that make the headlines: the big numbers with sales and list growth. With an external launch, you are looking to other sources besides just your own list to sell your course. The most obvious is Facebook Ads, but other sources such as being a podcast guest, LinkedIn Events, and partner promotions also work to drive in big numbers.

Inner Circle members Lou and Tami Santini were looking to multiply their reach and sales from their travel agency business. So when they launched a course meant to show other event planners and travel agents how to sell destination wedding travel, they were looking to generate big sales.

They knew that other wedding planning coaches would be a good fit because they were offering a new way for these planners to do business. Tami reached out to her contacts and landed several speaking engagement and guest blogging opportunities as a result. This helped to grow their list with their "right-fit" clients.

They then supplemented their list growth-building activities with Facebook Ads. And they've been very successful.

Even in this year that has been difficult for their industry, they've generated $109,000 so far just from course sales.

There is no "one size fits all" launch, but there is one that is right for you. Which do you see yourself launching next?

# 12

# THE POWERFUL SALES MACHINE

## From Course to Next Sale

**BACK WHEN I** had my marketing agency and I didn't know any better, I would show up to prospect meetings on time, wait for a prospect to show up, get frustrated when they didn't and do it again the next time. That was terrible positioning of my authority, a complete waste of time and I knew there had to be something better. Thankfully there was, and we still use some of the strategies we discovered back then.

The beauty of making a sale after someone has already enrolled in your course is that you have a someone who is not just a lead but a buyer to sell to. And, after you make the course, you have a few options of getting someone from the course to the high-ticket offer, whether that is a group coaching program, taking them on as a client or selling a product.

At the end of this chapter, I'll show you how to use a virtual event to make it happen, which is how we do it most of the time, but first, let's look at the many other ways to get prospects to the next level.

## HOW TO GET YOUR PROSPECT TO "YES"

The relationship between you and your clients doesn't end once you get folks in the virtual room of your course. Remember: The course isn't your end game. Getting your clients to join you on the scaled journey is the long game. You not only want them to buy your course, but to continue to want to be in your business ecosystem. Here are some of the best ways to get them to the next sale.

## SALES CALL AS A BONUS

One of the incentives we give to drive in a sales call is to have attendees choose the full-pay option instead of the payment plan. Those who choose to enroll in our program just to be able to get on the phone with me are incredible prospects. Many of the people who came into our coaching program came in through getting on this call with me.

## EMAIL CALLS TO ACTION

We leverage our email list with occasional calls to action to get on the phone with one of my salespeople. I write these emails as a tease to the prospect, and they book a call. My most recent Elite Client came into our coaching by asking for a call after reading an email.

Example of a call-to-action email:

> Tuesday May 31
>
> **Subject: Want to launch in just 42 days?**
>
> To all non-coaching members (can go to past members)
>
> (Name),
>
> When it comes to profitably scaling your business, the question I get asked most often is, "How quickly can I start generating revenue?"
>
> In the past, I've shared that our members who are fast action takers have launched within 42 days.
>
> But never before did we put together a blueprint showing you how...

Until now, that is.

The team and I crafted the "42 Days to Start Generating Revenue" Plan that you may use for your first launch or your next... as the fast path to success. We just gave it to our Power Up Members so that they can launch their first webinar and sell a digital course in less than a month and a half.

Curious to find out if Power Up Accelerators Club is right for you?

Book a call with one of our Power Coaches now to find out.

go.oncehub.com/OneonOnewithaPowerCoach (link to application)

But hurry, space is limited.

Cheers,

Kim "ROI Roadmap Creator" Walsh Phillips

## THE FACEBOOK GROUP

Prospects can book a call when they first enter the Facebook Group. We offer a free gift with a thank-you page offer to book a call often. This drives leads into a conversation with our sales team.

## FREE GIFT WHEN I AM A GUEST

When I am a guest on someone else's podcast, summit, or speaking event, I offer a free gift of our Audience Builder Blueprint, and on the thank-you page for that free gift we offer a chance to book a call with one of our coaches to see if we can work together.

## BONUS VIP BENEFIT

Whether it is someone who upgrades to VIP for an event experience or in a challenge we hold, those who spend more for VIP access are demonstrating that they are willing to invest in themselves to accomplish a goal. This makes them a great prospect for coaching. All of these VIP levels come with a one-on-one call with one of our coaches, driving in more qualified leads for sales conversation.

## CLOSING THE SALE

When it comes to consultants and coaches, the best of the best are busy, in demand, and have authority. Thankfully, there are a few things you can do to set that up for yourself before the prospect call.

First off, do not accept any prospect request and meet with that person sooner than 48 hours. You can't get on the phone with Mark Cuban the same day, and no one else should be able to do that with you, either. It will be hard to resist the urge to meet right away, but if a prospect won't wait that long, then they would most likely be a frustrating client, and it's best for you to know now.

Second, do not be the one to schedule your call. Utilize an assistant, leverage a service like Fancy Hands or simply by creating a Gmail account to serve as your "assistant." When you aren't the one scheduling your call, it creates more authority positioning for you.

Furthermore, speaking of scheduling, as I mentioned earlier—do not send the prospect your Calendly or Once Hub app with 3,421 open slots on it and tell the person to book. You hardly seem in demand when you do that. I'm not changing my mind. Scheduling your appointments is not a task a Powerful Professional does for themselves.

Finally, your prospect should receive a list of all of the questions you want to ask ahead of time, first so this person is not surprised that you are going to actually ask them relevant questions, but also so they realize your call is not just some type of dog and pony show.

## MY 7-FIGURE PROSPECTING FUNNEL

Here's what we do when a prospect requests an appointment:

1. Prospect requests appointment.
2. "Laurie" offers three dates and times to prospect and puts a hold on my calendar.
3. Once time is confirmed, "Laurie" sends questions email.
4. A copy of my book is overnight shipped from Amazon gift wrapped with a note that says, "Kim looks forward to your call on (date and time). I hope your meeting goes great!" –Laurie

5. "Laurie" confirms with prospect the day of the call.
6. Call starts on time on Zoom.
7. Kim mentions questions and goes through them.
    ➡ What are you hoping to accomplish with your call with Kim?
    ➡ What's the number one goal you have when it comes to coaching?
    ➡ Have you worked with a coach before? If so, how did it go?
    ➡ What is your current company revenue?
    ➡ It's a year from now and you are super happy we are working together. What needs to have happened in your business in order to make that statement true?
    ➡ It's a year from now and you were incredibly disappointed after we spent time working together. What would've happened to make that statement true?
    ➡ What else is important that we know about you and your goals?
    ➡ Looking forward to hearing about you and your business. If you have any questions in the meantime, please let me know.
8. Afterwards, send an email recap and a link to enroll.

## TONY ROBBINS, JEFF WALKER, RUSSELL BRUNSON... AND THE WOMAN BEHIND THEIR EVENTS

I have one rule about who I seek advice from: I only take it if I am willing to trade places with the person giving me that advice on the topic I am asking about.

As I was looking to scale, I wanted to host our first virtual event as I saw others doing. We had done in-person events before, and we had done virtual ones, but never in the way I saw them doing it. You can only figure out so much from the outside. I knew I needed help because I couldn't figure it all out on my own.

It was one thing to watch from the outside and something else entirely to know how it all worked.

Then I actually had a little God whisper on a Thursday, and I shared it with my husband on a walk. I wanted to find a coach to teach me how to run these kinds of virtual events. One that had a blueprint I could follow. On Friday, I listened to a podcast, Mixergy with Andrew Warner, that I hadn't listened to in years, but for some reason, that day, I tuned in.

I heard Bari Baumgardner being interviewed. She started SAGE Event Management, Inc. 16 years ago in a guest bedroom turned home office. She quickly became known for her "strategy first" approach to designing high-impact, high-converting events. From working with Glazer Kennedy Insider's Circle (founded by Dan Kennedy, the co-author of my first published book) to some of the biggest names in the speaker, author, and influencer industry—Dean Graziosi, Tony Robbins, Russell Brunson, Pedro Adeo, Mary Morrissey, Pete Vargas, Lisa Sasevich, Jeff Walker, Amy Porterfield, Stu McLaren, and others—she quickly became the go-to resource for her "sales is service" mindset and big events, many of which I had attended.

Bari was a guest on the show, and she was talking about virtual events. At the end of the episode, she made an invitation to join her on her virtual event. I was listening and saying out loud, "No way! Is this really the answer to my prayer right now?" I didn't know the event she was talking about was literally starting as I was hearing the podcast, so when I went to join the next day, it was already in progress. I got on there with one goal in mind—to join her coaching program.

When they made the offer, I quickly enrolled and nerded out on "all of the things" and started implementing, asking questions along the way as I needed help, and contributing to the community as I could.

Within 45 days of joining, I held our first virtual event from which we brought in almost half a million dollars in revenue and launched our group coaching program. Since then, we've done over $2 million in events. I went from being a coaching client to part of Bari's Expert Faculty, (I teach her clients how to scale and fill the room) and we encourage all of our clients to put on virtual events as part of their program.

I had a chance to interview Bari for this book and asked her how she got started. She shared that she's always loved creating events. It has been in her DNA since she was the kid in high school who planned the prom. When she figured out she could make money doing it, she went into the event planning industry.

Bari, like myself, is focused more on the outcome instead of the event. The purpose of the event is planned far ahead of time. Very much like the Winning Webinar, first you set the goal, then you create the strategy and then only afterword do you hold the event.

The great thing about webinars, masterclasses, summits, and one-day events is that once you know all the options, you can pick the best ones for you, and mix and match them. The goal is that you learn the model and structure, then find the thing that allows you to have real impact in this world.

Whether you're doing a virtual event, in-person, or hybrid, there's a whole new buffet of options courtesy of COVID. Most work whether you are holding them in person or virtually.

## CONQUERING THE FOUR BELIEFS

When I spoke with Bari, she shared this gem about belief: "The thing that stops most people in their tracks is being stuck in their heads about selling. Did you ever say, 'I love to serve, but if I'm really honest, I'm not sure about the selling'? A core concept for you to realize is that if your prospects are not enrolled in themselves, then why would they enroll with you? If they don't believe they can do whatever you have to offer, why would they pay you to help them do it? Of course, they're not going to buy if they don't believe the thing can work for them."

This is one of the foundational principals of an effective event, or really any marketing. We think of the thing that we sell, but what is required is a belief before buying. They have to know that they can before they will.

There are four beliefs to conquer when it comes to events. You will notice they are very similar to the four Winning Webinar beliefs you read about earlier. You need to get your prospect to believe:

1. **The solution you have is the ultimate solution to their problem.** We focus on what they want, not on what we do, and

we don't try to cover too much. We focus on one big problem that will be solved, and we repeat it throughout the event.

2. **You are the one to show them how to fix it.** Your audience needs to see social proof that you are capable of bringing someone success and they wouldn't be a guinea pig to try out your method. Social proof is what you share in the form of examples. Having your students share their case studies, show up as guest speakers, or be part of a success panel can demonstrate this.

3. **They can have success with your system/offer.** Most people come into an event with head trash and memories of moments that didn't go well in the past. A lot of your event will be spent dispelling their inner belief that they are not destined for success. I believe this is one of the greatest gifts you can give people through your event.

4. **Their inner circle believes in you and your offer.** The time you spend with your prospect is a grain of sand compared to the time they spend with others. Getting their inner circle of influencers involved from the start goes a long way in building rapport and trust. Bring-a-friend tickets, awards programs where they are encouraged to invite their friends and family to attend, and/or including a spouse or partner in your high-ticket offer are all ways to bring in their social circle.

When you walk your prospects through these four beliefs and ensure all content matches one of the four, then you easily walk your prospect into making the next best decision.

Bari shared, "With high-ticket offers, buyers come in two different forms. Your right-fit client either wants speed or handholding. Either you're allowing them to cut you a check for speed—not making mistakes along the way so they can get there faster, simpler, and easier, or they're asking for you to hold their hand while they get there, providing some form of accountability and support. Ideally, your high-ticket offer does both. So if they run into an obstacle, they don't stay stuck. Why wouldn't they want that kind of service?"

Imagine what you could do if you could double, triple, or 10X a webinar, masterclass, launch, challenge, course, or membership. All of that is possible through the power of using a live event as a vehicle to make your high-ticket offer.

Bari says, "Serving one-to-one is a great strategy, confirming your concept, getting to know your right-fit client. It's how I started my business. But going from one-to-one into one-to-many—selling one time to reach more people—is the difference in being on calls 365 days a year to enroll 365 clients versus a 3-day event that makes an offer and sells so that you can serve for 362 days. Most people who come to me love serving. 'If I could sell for three days and serve for 362, that would be magic!'"

## KNOW YOUR EVENT VALUE

Let's talk about the difference between low-ticket and high. Bari places that dividing line at $6k based on her industry experience. Anything under $6k is low-ticket. Anything above that is high-ticket.

Your decision can be based on how quickly most people will be able to make the decision to join your program. For low-ticket offers, your prospects are quickly able to say yes and sign up. But for a high-ticket offer, the more money it costs, the more likely logical buyers will need to time to percolate on it. They will ask themselves questions like: *Is this right for me? Is this the right time for me? Is this the right mentor for me? Is this the right community for me? Can I afford to do this right now?* So high-ticket takes a little bit more decision time.

Now, admittedly, depending on your audience, maybe $4k is still high-ticket. That may be true for you, so run this through your own filter, based on your location, who you are serving, and that mindset muscle we're building.

No matter how you do it, an event is a much quicker way to make a high-ticket offer than doing individual one-to-one sales. One of my favorite things about them is that it allows me to serve an entire audience while creating massive profits.

Our first three-day event was focused on launching courses, and we had about 100 people attend. I did that event from my basement with a brand-new puppy at home. A crazy combination, not for the faint at heart, especially as Daisy chewed through my light box cord minutes before I made my offer.

That didn't stop us from having a successful event, with 32 of the attendees joining our brand-new coaching program.

Since then, we've changed the focus of our events from courses to the overall scaling model of our business—with courses being an option, but not a requirement to scale after several of our coaching members were able to use our model without a course.

## KNOW YOUR EVENT MODEL

We've also condensed the three-day model to one day and continue to have the same success. It's much less taxing on my team and myself, with a lot less expense. I now prefer it over the three-day model.

Our One-Day Model works like this:

| TIME | DETAILS | PURPOSE |
|------|---------|---------|
| 10:45 a.m. | Doors open, chat roll on, music playing. | Create excitement, engagement and give people time to show up. |
| 11:00 a.m. | Someone welcomes with high energy, tells attendees to turn camera on, and goes through event resources, then introduces you. | Set up expectations of the day. Puts you in charge; Gives time for people to show up. |
| 11:05 a.m. | Welcome; Highlight content of day; Intro to you with case studies woven in; Example of how mistakes of the past prepared you for today; Have them realize their past mistake and how it prepared them, then share in small group; Share back in the main group. | |
| 12:00 p.m. | Letter one of framework. | Get them feeling value so they want to come back from break. |

| | | |
|---|---|---|
| 12:30 p.m. | 15-minute break with music. | Stretch, stand up, keep energy high. |
| 12:45 p.m | Prizes back from break; Letter one to letter two of framework; Takeaway and share. | See the possibilities of the system. |
| 2:15 p.m. | Lunch break | |
| 2:45 p.m. | Welcome back from lunch with energy movement and prizes; Letters two, three and four; Remove head trash. | See the possibilities of the system; Remove obstacles. |
| 4:15 p.m. | 15-minute break with music. | Stretch, stand up, keep energy high. |
| 4:30 p.m. | Hot content; Inspiration panel; Offer. | Excited for offer; See how it's possible. |
| 6:00 p.m. | Dinner break | Enrollment lobby to sell. |
| 6:30 p.m. | "On the fence answers" and clarifications; Q&A; Emotional appeal close. | See the possibilities of the system. |
| 7:30 p.m. | Event over/enrollment lobby open. | Keep sales going. |

And if you are considering a virtual event, the next questions in your mind are likely granular:

➡ What do I call it?
➡ How do I price it?
➡ What's the secret to filling it?

Bari shared, "I think of Apex Accelerator as the path for your right-fit client—coming up from free to a low-ticket item, to a live event, to a high-ticket item. It's not a zigzag. It's just a matter of how much they want to spend and how much access they get to you. When we look at that, it really demystifies the whole profit pyramid concept."

## GOING FOR THE HIGH-TICKET OFFER

As I outlined in Chapter 6, everything starts with free.

Your Alex or Ally finds you on social media, podcasts, challenges, launches, webinars, and masterclasses.

This leads to your webinar, and your webinar sells them a course. The course comes with a ticket to your virtual event. Some charge a refundable deposit to ensure their audience attends, others a materials fee to get an upfront commitment, and still others just make it free.

Some of our coaching clients don't have a course or like us, they supplement their course buyers by also doing a webinar to go straight to ticket sales. We price our one-day ticket at $197 and it works well for us. I've seen pricing by others from $47 up to $2,500.

Bari shared, "From the live event comes the high-ticket offer you're going to make. On average, it's for group coaching in the $10-15k range, masterminds in the $25k range, or private VIP days for $20k and up. You might be thinking, *Well, I want to do a mastermind, but I'm not ready to charge $25k.* No problem. You just charge less. Once you build that mindset muscle, you can raise the rates. Maybe start at $7,500, then $10k, then $15k, and later $25k.

"And if we say that all roads lead to your high-ticket offer—regardless of what that high-ticket offer actually is, its price point, or format—you can be super intentional in everything you do to attract your right-fit client. This is someone who is going to pay you more for greater access as they go. Knowing this, how can you package, position, and price your high-ticket offer? And if you're thinking, *I'm not ready yet*, then I want you to just guess. What do you currently charge? How many people can you serve per day with that? Just do quick math. Keep it top level. Then based on what you're learning here, what could you charge for your high-ticket offer?"

Not everyone is at the same place in their journey or industry. If $4,000 is your high-ticket offer, that's great. How many people could you serve in a year with that high-ticket offer? Look at how much you earn through low-ticket offers and how many people you can serve compared to how much you can make and how many people can you serve with high-ticket offerings.

No doubt you're going to earn more on high-ticket but you're also going to serve more deeply to the high-ticket clients. Now if you can put those two paths together, your right-fit client will say, "That was awesome. I want more." Then it's a win for you and a win for your right-fit client.

So, what is a high-ticket offer? On a really high level, it means people paying more money to get faster results focused on what your clients need most from you. Here are some examples:

➡ It could be group coaching like our Power Up Accelerators Club program, a mastermind like our Inner Circle Mastermind, or more done-for-you like our Inner Circle Elite level.

➡ It might be investing in a real estate fund like one of our client's offers or becoming a client of a law practice, or even purchasing a $250,000 curriculum package like yet another one of our clients offers.

➡ It can even be simpler, like a retreat where you take a deep dive into one topic and get something done—an adult version of summer camp where instead of sunburn and friendship bracelets you come home with things done.

Bari shared, "Typically a high-ticket offer is going to have multiples of these. It might be that I offer two retreats or an implementation day every other month, plus a mastermind meetup every quarter. Once you know the format and delivery, then you can decide the rhythm of how often. It's really that simple."

If you had to guess right now, which options appeal to you most as you're just starting to design your high-ticket offer? What price point would you offer it at, and how would you serve your market?

Bari shared, "If you look at the rhythm of your ideal mix, every so often there's meeting for a deep, immersive experience, combined with periodic meetings for a quick hit to keep everyone connected and moving, supplemented with a daily opportunity to connect with the community. If you've been making high-ticket offers super complicated, stop."

Keep it simple. You can think of a high-ticket offer as two things:

**ACE: Accountability, Community, Enhanced Opportunity**
**RIM: Repetition, Immersion, Modeling**

She suggests, "Accountability helps people get things done. A like-minded community makes people feel supported and part of something bigger. Enhanced opportunity allows your member to be more, do more, have more, and make more. But it's not always about just making more money. In your industry it might be helping people make more love, make more light, or make more health. It works the same way across the continuum from personal development to business development. Repetition lets people try things over and over until they gain confidence. Immersion allows them to soak in the learning. Modeling demonstrates proven practices because your members don't want to reinvent the wheel. ACE is what you deliver, and RIM is how you deliver it."

Your high-ticket offer will ideally include some form of accountability, community, and enhanced opportunity. How you deliver it is through repetition, immersion, and modeling proven practices—things you've already figured out, so that they're not reinventing the wheel, just following the formula. That's part of what they're paying for.

## ⏻ GET TO KNOW RIM

*Let's take a closer look at a great way to make a lasting impact with your right-fit client: RIM (Repetition, Immersion, Modeling). This example is courtesy of my friend Bari, whom you met earlier, in her words.*

Let's say your business is about health, wealth, and happiness. So, you're going to hold a two-day health retreat where you're going to implement ideas on health. Then you're going to have a two-day wealth retreat where you're going to implement ideas on wealth. And you're going to follow those up with a two-day happiness retreat where you're going to implement ideas on happiness. Every four months you're going to come together for two days and work on one considerably important topic and then move on to the next. Over the course of a year, your members will be able to repeat it, become immersed in it, and model it, so that at the end of the year they have mastery over their health, wealth, and happiness. You'll also include monthly hot seats, monthly Q&A calls, and a Facebook group.

If that's your high-ticket offer, now you know your destination. Lock that into your GPS for where you're going. Now what's the fastest path to get there? You want to take the highway with no traffic, the path with the least number of turns, and the one where you're allowed to drive the fastest. Remember: The goal is to make the shift into this new anti-hustle-and-grind model for your business.

How will you leverage the first sale to get to your next sale, then to consistent sales? That's RIM—repetition, immersion, modeling. I want you to get super comfortable in that through real-life experience.

The first thing you want to do is ignite your audience with a launch, challenge, masterclass, summit, or webinar. What you offer for free is kind of like the Costco/BJ's/Sam's Club sampler. On Saturdays they put out free samples so you can taste everything and then when you like it, they ask, "Would you like more?" When you answer, "Heck, yeah," they say, "Well, great. It's right here. Would you like one box or two?"

Now, do I feel sold by that Costco employee when that happens? No. Do I find myself thinking, *I cannot believe they offered me that free thing on the skewer and then had the gall to ask me if I wanted more of it just because I liked it. Can you believe this shakedown at Costco?* No. Honestly, I'm like, "Yeah, can I have another? I won't tell anybody. Then I'll take two boxes."

That's how it works. You serve something up for free so your right-fit clients can fall in love with it and want more. Think of your business that way.

The thing you're going to have to tackle is that you only have so much time to devote to serving for free. You need to identify one problem and one solution, and you're going to have to tackle that mindset muscle because it's the thing that's most likely to stand in your way and in your right-fit client's way. You want to teach on a very high level. Your presentation is not the deep-dive.

Think again about the Costco samples. What if after you tried the sample and loved it, the employee said, "You like that? Fantastic. Let me walk you back to the kitchen and show you how they make this. I'm going to show you exactly how we grow it, then how we cut it up and chop it, and then how we turn it into a... "

You'd likely reply, "No, I actually don't want that. I've got an appointment in an hour. I just want two boxes to take home." Remember you're not trying to give your right-fit clients everything in your presentation. You're trying to keep it super high level, because if you do a great job of that, they are going to say, "That was amazing. I love what you taught me on health, wealth, and happiness. I had big *a-has* around each of those concepts. I want more."

Then you can say, "Fantastic," and go into a deeper dive—the equivalent of putting boxes into their cart. "If you love this, then you're also going to love the eight-week course I have where we go even deeper on the problems, the solutions, and building your mindset muscle. I'm going to have two whole weeks on health, two whole weeks on wealth, and two whole weeks on happiness."

And if you're wondering what happened to weeks 1 and 8, the first is the onboarding and welcome week, and the last is the graduation and celebration week. An eight-week course can literally be that simple, and in fact it should be—no zigging or zagging.

What's going to happen at the end of the course if you do an amazing job? They're going to say, "That was great, I want more." And you're going to say, "Awesome, I thought you might because you're my right-fit client. The good news is there's even more. In fact, I'm holding an event soon. If you liked what I gave free, and you loved what I did in this course, then you are going to really love spending time at this live event with me where we tackle—even deeper—more problems, more solutions, and really go to work on that mindset muscle. Things you thought you couldn't accomplish, you absolutely can during this event, so join me, and we're going to spend a whole day on health and a whole day on wealth, and a whole day on happiness."

What's going to happen during that three-day event? Because you're going to give generously and go even deeper on these topics, what are they going to say afterward? They want more! And who are you not to give it to them?

What if you took them through your free offering, then your course and live event, and when they said, "That was awesome! I would love more!" you reply, "Nope, that's all I got." That's like enjoying a Costco sample when there are no boxes left to take home. That's just cruel.

Of course you want to have the next step ready for them, and here's where you make a high-ticket offer. You're going to invite them to spend more time with you, so that they can have ACE—accountability, community, and enhanced opportunity—so they can develop RIM—repetition, immersion, and modeling. They're going to need both to gain mastery. Your other offerings are part of the learning process. It opens their minds. For people like "the hare," who are fast movers, that might be just enough. For those types of customers, you can be happy they came to your three-day event and got what they needed. After all, they are likely to rave about the event, come back again, and bring other people with them next time.

Your high-ticket offer won't be for everyone. You're not going to say, "But if you want the keys to the kingdom, *you've got to buy this*." That would feel icky. What you must realize is that people will understand you are giving as much as you can for the level of what they're paying.

What would happen if I took a year's worth of information and tried to pack it into a three-day event? Have I served my audience, or have I just totally overwhelmed them? It's your job to filter your teachings of what they need and when they need it and how much they need of it so that they will be able to use it most effectively.

Like the Costco sample, are they going to give you a whole cake at the end of the aisle, or are they going to give you just one bite? A bite is enough, making sure they get a bit of cake, a bit of icing, and some of the little diddly-dobs on top.

I want your offer to be that perfect bite so your right-fit clients will keep saying, "That was amazing. I want more."

But you can't offer some people cake, some people icing, and some people diddly-dobs. That's not going to be the perfect experience that makes anyone want more. Your job is to put your knowledge and skills through that filter of thinking through what's the right way for your right-fit clients to consume content so they want more. You absolutely want them to be able to use it, so that they rave, and they renew, and they recruit.

Then when it's time for the high-ticket offer, you can invite them to join you. "We're going to work on your problems and your solutions, and we're going to build that mindset muscle so that you have real clarity and real confidence and real results by the end of the (six months or year, or whatever your program length is)."

Now it's time to decide what your high-ticket offer really looks like. Does it include a two-day retreat plus monthly hot seats, monthly Q&As, and a daily Facebook group?

Once you know the destination and build everything out to lead your right-fit prospects to that destination, then you can be super intentional in everything you do to get them there. It doesn't matter if it's a podcast, 10-minute stage time, or someone asks you a question on Clubhouse. When your ascension plan is in place, everyone is rowing the boat in the same direction. You don't want one of your offerings to row the front of the boat to the right, but another offering at the back of the boat to be rowing to the left. You'd just go in circles. But when everything is rowing in the same direction, you get across that lake faster, simpler, and easier. That's what you want to do with your marketing and with every intentional thing you do to get there. That's how you go from a first sale to next sale, and then to consistent sales where your purpose-driven payday is.

To lay this out in the order, first you focus on your right-fit client, building authority, celebrity, and expert status. Then you scale quickly with a Client Generation Machine, where you turn your current clients into an unpaid sales force. Then you make the offer and any bonus.

This takes you and individual selling out of the equation. Can you still do one-on-one calls? Of course you can, but this gives you leverage of time and resources to be able to bring many people in at one time and because of the way you engage them and make them an offer, they move quicker through the stages of your Apex Accelerator.

If you are worried that someone is already selling in your industry and the market is "saturated," Bari coaches, "No one can do it the way you do. A solid benefit of group coaching is letting your members see you solve others' problems in real-time. You're not going to find that anywhere else. Your right-fit members will be attracted to your way of doing it—your unique lens, humor, style, process, and method. When they see you in action, they'll think, 'That's who I want to learn from!'"

She continues, "The reality is there are a lot of people teaching live events. That doesn't mean yours won't be uniquely useful. Do you know that every song is made up of the same eight notes? Every book falls into one of 20 master plots. What makes a song or book unique is the inflection of the voice, the style and the vision of the person delivering it. Stephen King is different than Dean Koontz. Danielle Steele is different than Nicholas Sparks. The Rolling Stones and John Mayer are both successful, but with two completely different styles—using the same exact equipment, and the same exact notes.

"There's abundance, not a diminishing supply. No one is stealing your audience. Be authentically you and show up as you. Don't take other people's stuff. Do your own thing, and I promise you people will love you because you're just so authentic."

We are change makers. We know that our unique ability really does change the world. One event at a time, one attendee at a time. The little ripple effects do their job. The world has never needed you more than it needs you right now. The world is craving leadership, solutions, and someone brave enough to say, "I know how to do this, and I can show you how. Let me light the way!"

You can do this, and the starting point is not waiting for everything to be perfect. It is about getting started with the very first step and moving up your Apex Accelerator. The whole thing does not need to be fully fleshed out before you get started, nor should it be. You will be able to form it along the way as you ask your clients for insights on what they need and how you can best serve them.

Before we move onto the next chapter all about crafting your high-ticket offer, here is an exercise for you to complete.

##  POWER EXERCISE

What belief has held you back from making your first or next high-ticket offer?

Take a minute and think about it. What is the thing?

*If I were thinner... if I were younger... if I didn't have those wrinkles... if I hadn't gained 10 pounds during COVID... if I had the perfect outfit... If I had a bigger team... if I had more clarity... if I had more money... if I had a bigger list... if I had a bigger TV or better computer...*

What's holding you back? Write it here:

_____

Now what belief has held you back from creating your first or next event? This may or may not be the same answer. The previous question was about making an offer, while this one asks you about taking that stage where you will eventually make the offer.

What do you need in order to get confident so you can have your own purpose-driven payday? What is the gap you need to close?

What do you need before your belief in your service so outweighs your fear of the sale? Your right-fit prospects need you.

So what do you have to do to close that gap? Write it here:

_____

**Stop dreaming about it and start doing it.**

Events are a big part of how you can impact the world and generate revenue to stop relying on one-on-one calls. This may just be the piece missing from scaling your business. In the next chapter we will dive into what to develop as your high-ticket offer the founder with my friend Scott Whitaker of Membership Multipliers.

# 13

# MAKING YOUR HIGH-TICKET OFFER

## By Scott Whitaker

**THERE ARE TWO** challenges that people face when it comes to crafting their high-ticket offer. One is obvious and the other is more hidden. The obvious challenge is the one that people think is holding them back, when in reality it's the hidden challenge that is the root problem of crafting and selling your high-ticket offer.

What are they? The obvious challenge is knowing what to include in your high-ticket offer. The hidden challenge is believing someone will actually pay you for it.

In this chapter, we're going to cover both! It's one thing for me to share what to include in your high-ticket offer, but you will have far more success if you also believe that you can and will be paid for it.

## COMPONENTS OF THE HIGH-TICKET OFFER

Regardless of what you're going to provide your members, in the end, they all want the same thing, and there are a number of people who will pay top dollar to get it.

Here's what to include in your high-ticket offer:

## SPEED

"Money buys speed." I'm not sure who said it first, but it's true. Many people desire speed so they can accomplish their goals faster.

Kim did this. She hired me for a VIP Day where we went to work on crafting her high-ticket offers. She invested $10,000 to spend the day focusing on how she could help more people. It also happened that she had an upcoming event where she planned to unveil this opportunity to those in attendance.

Her $10,000 investment in the VIP Day turned into over $127,000 in sales of her high-ticket offer. And it all happened in less than 12 days. Would you be willing to invest $10,000 so that you could create over $127,000 in sales? Who wouldn't?

Even if you don't provide a financial outcome for your clients, they still want speed. Whether it's relational, health, wellness, clarity, focus, or some intangible outcome, people still desire to get it and get it FAST.

## PERSONALIZATION

You may already have a course or some offering where you're able to help people on a broader scale. Don't forget those who are currently investing in your offer but would be willing to invest at a higher level if they could get a customized plan . . . a way to have you directly tell them what they should do based on your expertise.

Everyone who invests in Kim's Power Up Accelerators Club receives a customized blueprint on how they can grow and scale their business. Even if they don't have an offer yet.

This is part of Kim's "unique genius." She's now crafted the framework for hundreds of her members in numerous niches. She's able to craft this personalized framework so that her members can serve more people.

I'm confident that as an expert in your field—even if you don't believe you are—you can customize your "unique genius" to help others gain the outcome that they desire.

## ACCESS TO YOU

Further up among Kim's high-ticket membership offers is her Inner Circle Elite. One of the many benefits of being in the Inner Circle Elite is that you receive direct access to Kim. Yes, you get to meet with her one-on-one. Members can bring their questions, challenges, and opportunities and get direct guidance from her.

This level of access is usually reserved for the highest levels of membership, simply because there's only so much time available to have these one-on-one meetings.

You can offer this access by:

➡ Fast Implementation Calls (given to new members to help them get started right)

➡ Weekly one-on-one calls (minimum 20 minutes but no longer than 60)

➡ Monthly one-on-one calls (minimum 20 minutes but no longer than 60)

➡ Every other week calls (minimum of 20 minutes but no longer than 60)

➡ Voice messaging or text messaging (using online apps like Voxer)

➡ Open office hours where all members are invited to show up and ask their questions

You can even mix and match the opportunities so that you can scale your business without having to "grind" and become a "slave to Zoom."

## ACCESS TO TOOLS AND RESOURCES

Are there tools or resources you could provide that would help enhance your high-ticket membership offer? Make a list.

Every high-ticket membership offer that Kim and I have crafted together came through the process of creating a list. You can do the same.

Just answer these simple questions:

- What tools or resources do you have that you could provide to your high-ticket members?
- What tools or resources do other people have that you could give to your high-ticket members?
- What tools or resources, if you had enough members, could you buy for your high-ticket members?
- What tools or resources should you provide for members so they don't get stuck?

Don't limit your thinking to just technology. People are a resource for you! It just so happens that in Kim's high-ticket membership, I'm one of those resources where I provide coaching on how to create, launch, and sell high-ticket membership offers. Her members get access to me as a resource.

And not just me. They also get access to someone who will help set up their technology for them. After hearing from her members, Kim realized they were getting stuck because they couldn't set up some of their tech, so she created a shortcut for them and hired someone to do it for them. Which leads us to the next opportunity you have...

## "DONE FOR YOU"

This suggestion comes with a word of caution: Make sure your "done for you" services are scalable. Otherwise, you'll be hustling and grinding instead of experiencing the freedom that comes with serving people through a high-ticket offer.

"Done for you" doesn't mean "done by you." You don't have to be the one providing the service. You can outsource it. You can hire someone and make them part of your team. If it doesn't fall in your area of expertise, then get someone else to do it for your members.

A good litmus test on whether or not you should consider providing "done for you" is to answer the question, "Will this help my members get unstuck?" If the answer is yes, then it's a good reason for you to find a way for them to have "done for you" as part of your high-ticket offer.

Don't make the mistake of thinking that if you add "done for you" it will create more value and you'll be able to charge more. It might. But the odds are against you because you will have an offer that you can't scale, is too dependent on an external source or individual, and/or will decrease the profit margin on your offer.

That's why I like...

## "DONE WITH YOU"

This can be scaled. After all, it's "one to many" (not "one-on-one"). "Done with you" comes with the benefit of everyone in your high-ticket offer having the ability to learn from one another.

Inside Kim's high-ticket membership offer, members have the opportunity to design a webinar to sell their services, programs, courses, and memberships. She has a proven "done with you" process so that members who desire to use a webinar can do so and at the same time learn from others who are working on the same thing.

When a member launches their webinar, everyone gets to learn from that member plus Kim as she guides them through the blueprint. It's a great opportunity to provide collective thinking and feedback for her members.

You can do the same. As you take your members through your coaching, they will learn from both you and other members as everyone is walking alongside one another and you're "doing it with them" every step of the way.

## CONVENIENCE

People pay for convenience. Convenience stores mark up their price so that you don't have to deal with the hassle of going to the grocery store. Everything is marked up. Why? Because they know that guys like me don't want to deal with walking through the aisles looking for that one thing when they can go right into the convenience store and be in and out in under five minutes. It's convenient!

- ➡ How can you make the outcome of your membership convenient?
- ➡ Can you simplify the steps?
- ➡ Can you make it easier to understand?

- → Can you provide less frustration?
- → Can you enable your members to add their staff, spouse, or other team members so they don't have tell others what you told them?

One of the ways Kim has included this in her high-ticket offer is by having a monthly training session where her COO, Kelly LeMay, leads a training session for those in the operations role. Kelly will train in operations so that you don't have to train your team member on operations.

When you take these seven opportunities that are available to you and combine them with the value you know you're already able to provide your members, you can see how easy it becomes to create your high-ticket offer.

You can mix and match these seven opportunities or include them all. Just know that "more doesn't always mean **more!**" Simply by adding more to your offer doesn't mean that you can then charge more. It needs to be balanced with the outcome that your members desire.

You don't want your members to feel like they're paying for benefits they'll never use. Take the right combination that is going to get your members the best outcome and you'll have the right offer.

## GETTING PAID FOR YOUR HIGH-TICKET OFFER

Now that you know what to include in your high-ticket offer, let's focus on getting paid. You must believe that people will pay for your high-ticket offer.

**"Your belief that people will pay for your high-ticket offer precedes people paying for it."**

Would you be willing to believe that some people may not sign up for your offer because you didn't charge enough? It almost happened to me. It was a meeting in Nashville, TN, with a number of entrepreneurs. It just so happened that Kim was there, too. We were all sharing about our business and learning from one another. One of the members, Mike

Agugliaro, took his turn and started to present. He shared how he had just sold his service business for eight figures and was now going to focus on his coaching business, CEO Warrior.

He began to share his plan for his coaching business, and to be honest, the plan had a number of holes and wasn't likely to succeed as he desired. I shared with Mike a few tips on what he could do to impact more people. He asked, "How can we work together?"

I shared my process but knew there was no way I could charge him what I was charging others. He was at a different level. It was in that moment that I doubled my price. I quoted him this higher figure and he said, "Let's do it."

Since then, Mike has utilized my services numerous times. During one of our meetings, I asked him, "If I had told you the price was half of what I charged you that day, would you have still said yes?"

"No!" he answered. "I wouldn't have thought it was worth my time."

That was the day I doubled my price. It's also the day I realized there were probably people who had previously told me, "No!" just because my price wasn't high enough.

Why didn't I price it that high to begin with? Because I didn't believe people would pay me for it. My belief that people would pay high-ticket prices had to precede me charging high-ticket prices.

Everyone has limiting beliefs. I have them, Kim has them, and no doubt you have them too. But that's why you need people who are going to push you to grow. That's one of the reasons I enjoy working with Kim. She sees the areas where I'm limiting my impact and limiting my ability to help others because of my negative thinking. Then she gives me the opportunity to challenge her limiting beliefs as well.

There's a wise saying, "As iron sharpens iron, so one person sharpens another." You need a network of people who have the goal of making you sharp—people who will build you up and challenge your limiting beliefs, people who will believe in your ability in spite of your own doubts.

There's another wise saying, "Why do you look at the speck of sawdust in your brother's eye and pay no attention to the plank in your own?"

Sometimes you need people who are going to call out the planks in your eye when you're looking at the sawdust in theirs.

It's easy to call out the negative thinking in others. Having someone call out your own negative thinking is of greater value. If you would like to learn more about how Kim can help do this for you, go to TheShiftBookBonus.com to connect with her and get all of the bonuses that are included with this book.

But you're still probably wondering . . .

### How much should I charge?

Everyone wants me to tell them how much to charge. It's one of the most common questions I get. And usually they already know. They just want me to give them the confidence that it's possible.

You can have the confidence too just by answering a few simple questions:

- ➡ Can you add a **zero** to your current offer? Maybe you have an online course, that you're selling for $997. Can you add a zero and offer a high-ticket membership program for $9,970? Just take the content of your course and add in a few of the above suggestions then add a zero.

- ➡ Can you double your price? That's what we did with Kim's Inner Circle Elite offer. It's double the investment of her Power Up Accelerators Club. Both are high-ticket offers; they just have different benefits and attract a different member.

- ➡ Does the new price of your high-ticket offer make you feel uncomfortable? If you answered, "**yes!**" to that question, then good! You probably have an offer that is high enough for the time being. Just know that as soon people begin to take your offer, you'll become comfortable with it, and you may need to increase your price again. If you answered, "**no!**" to that question, or had any hesitation in your answer, then you're probably not charging enough. The amount you charge should at some level, make you feel uncomfortable. This discomfort will give you the desire to make sure you provide the most value and best outcome for your members. That discomfort will be the challenge that is set before you to make sure that your members get a good return on their investment.

➡ Does the price of your high-ticket offer provide the outcome *your members* desire **and** give you the freedom and margin to live the life *you desire*? This book is about saying no to the hustle-and-grind culture for a reason. The goal is to help you leverage the opportunities you have, provide extreme value to your members, give them the outcome they desire... and get paid for it. What good is it to have your own business only to become a slave to it? Yes, you should provide value to your members, and that value should correspond with the investment they're making in your high-ticket offer.

➡ Avoid proportionate thinking! What is proportionate thinking? Proportionate thinking comes from believing that "If my members make $100,000 then I should be able to charge 10 percent." Proportionate thinking comes into play any time you correspond the investment with the potential outcome. When it comes to setting up your offer, you'll want to avoid this. Why? Because every member is different. Some members will gain more, and some will gain less. Plus, you'll want to stay away from making income promises. That will help you avoid numerous legal nightmares. It's okay to have that amount as a goal. I do! I want my high-ticket members to add at least six figures in the first year and seven figures in the second or third year of our working together. But that's my goal for them. And many times, I don't even share that number with them. My goal for them has nothing to do with the amount that I charge them.

➡ Name your price! Right now! Do it! Name your price! If I was sitting across from you and had my credit card in hand ready to pay, what would you charge me? Don't put this off any longer! Why wait until you're talking with someone to figure out your price? Why wait until you have all the answers to name your price? Your price could be the key to helping you create your high-ticket offer. So before you move on to the next chapter, name your price.

 **POWER EXERCISE**

> Your price could be the key to helping you create your high-ticket offer. So before you move on to the next chapter, name your price.

## NOW THAT YOU HAVE A HIGH-TICKET OFFER

Scott did an incredible job of walking you through your high-ticket offer. One thing to remember is that people will pay your more, to get less content from you. They don't want a bunch of options. They want the one option that will get the job done.

Case in point...

Recently a few girlfriends and I went to one of my favorite restaurants. The waiter was a master salesperson because as he greeted us, he shared what his favorite cocktails are and things he enjoys most on the menu.

Let's be real. It was late. Our desire to enjoy a cocktail and dinner was strong. Yet, our desire to think was low. We were tired and just wanted to relax and enjoy.

So what did we do? Almost all of us chose a cocktail and menu item he suggested. He walked us right to the sale by taking away choice fatigue.

## SERVE THEM BY MAKING THE OFFER

Recently I got to do one of my favorite things we do at Powerful Professionals. I led a new group of Power Up Coaching members through the Client Generation Machine workshop where they picked their target market, the problem they were going to solve, and the steps they would take to solve them.

We finished the workshop with me writing their headline and creating the framework for each of them so they can quickly launch and generate sales.

Before we ended the meeting, I asked those who were willing to share why they were glad they were there. Person after person shared that they felt seen and heard, and that they finally got what they had always been looking for. They thought this program would be good, but not as good as it actually was.

I am not saying this to brag. I am saying this to teach a lesson, a really important one. None of them thought it would be as good as it was, so the only way I could really get them to experience it was to try it.

How could I do that? By taking away the commitment necessary in order to do so.

Most of the people in our coaching program have been in someone else's program in the past and were screwed over a time or two and are skeptical of doing it again.

We aren't like those programs, but there is no reason for someone to believe that. I have to get them to try our program, and one way we do this is that we don't have contracts. You join our membership and I earn your membership month after month. You stay because you want to be there. Yet, I've had members in coaching for more than seven years.

This is just one of the ways we get those who have been burned before to take a chance. How can you show up differently to your market? Is there something your competitors do that you could do differently?

And before you allow yourself to say, "I can't do that," or "That won't work in my field," pause and ask yourself, "How could I make this work for me and my market?"

Most would say they couldn't operate without a contract. To that, I ask, "Why not?" If you had a coaching client come to you who said they couldn't afford the program, you would always let that person out of it. So if that is the case, then why have the contract in the first place?

If you could take away the thing that frustrates your right-fit client most about your industry and use it as a competitive advantage, what might that look like?

If you don't know, simply ask your audience. Find out from them what is working and what isn't, then get creative in finding a solution that doesn't comprise your non-negotiables. Start there to reach more and multiply your impact and income.

In the next section, we will dive into how to make it easy, always and to stop being proud of doing hard things.

## THE STUPID BADGE OF HONOR

I used to be so proud of something so stupid. In my mind I was someone who thought, "I can do hard things" and then would think of the hard things I did as proof of the even harder things I could do. While that is better than thinking I couldn't do anything, this thought was not serving me.

Thinking of what I needed to do as hard did not serve me well. At all.

So I made a shift. What if my days didn't have to be hard? What if my days could actually be *easy*?

Here's where you take a hot minute to exhale because things are about to get easier. When I realized this, I switched my thinking to "How can I make this easy for myself?" And with that, everything changed.

When I thought that way about work, my kids, my diet, my exercise, everything felt lighter and more manageable. Everything. From drinking more water each day (buying a two-liter mug that I can keep at my desk), to getting 10,000 steps a day in (parking farther from my destinations and taking Daisy for a stroll while my girls are at softball practice), to batching content creation so I have a go-to bank of client attracting posts ready to go at all times.

Focusing on the easy made it all so much more doable.

Instead of, "I can do hard things," I switched to, "I make achieving my goals easy and fun."

I used this same philosophy when figuring out how to go from six figures to seven in a business model that I could map out for my coaching members.

It's simple:

- ➡ 1 webinar with about 30 opt-ins a day = **210 opt-ins a week**
- ➡ 20% will show up to the webinar = **42 show ups**
- ➡ 10% will buy your course, 4 sales @ $1,497 each = **$5,988**

- ➡ Of those 4, a third will progress to your group coaching program at $14,997, for 1.32 sales = **$19,796.04**
- ➡ Weekly revenue = **$25,784.04**
- ➡ Yearly revenue = **$1,340,770.08**

Yes, seriously. From 30 opt-ins a day, homing in on what each step requires, and then what it provides to the next level, when you start focusing on the small steps that get you to the big results, everything seems easier to achieve.

What's one thing you can make easy today with intention? Start that to not only scale your business, but to not burn out while doing so.

Speaking of easy, in the next chapter we'll flip criticism from being a negative to a positive so you can serve more powerfully.

# 14

# POWERFULLY POURING FUEL ON THE FIRE

## Powering On Your Impact and Income Multiplier

**REMEMBER BACK TO** the very beginning of this book when we talked about non-negotiables? One of ours is that if you are mean to me or my team, you are not invited to be part of our community. We don't allow cheap jerk-faces in.

After I refunded a student who was mean to my team, I had immense gratitude for having enough lead flow to be able to pick and choose who we work with, so I shared that story with my list.

That one email got me more unsubscribes than any other I've ever written!

And it's the best thing that ever happened.

It sorted out the people who aren't my right-fit clients. It also rose to the top those who are. You see, while it had the most unsubscribes from any email ever, it also had the highest open rates and response rate, with a 30-percent open rate and 2-percent click-through rate.

Even better, I heard story after story from those who had cheered when they got to let go a difficult client. I received other emails sharing the pain people were currently facing when wanting to let go of a client but couldn't do it yet.

I could engage and respond, spending time serving those who are a good fit to work with. That's exactly what good marketing should do.

Here's my challenge for you after reading this book. Every time you check your unsubscribes this week or get a negative comment online, celebrate! Jump for joy, pour a glass of bubbly, and just celebrate. Because that means you have been doing marketing that filters out those who aren't a good match. You will have more time to focus on those who are.

This mindset shift will allow you to be bolder and more authentic in your beliefs, views, and authenticity, enabling real connection with your tribe. People can only fall in love with you if you are yourself, after all.

And those who don't like it? Not your problem. There's a line behind them waiting.

Know that when you get three negatives, you are positively doing exactly what you are supposed to do.

So get out that bottle of bubbly and celebrate. Your tribe is waiting.

## MOVING FORWARD, EVEN WHEN YOU'RE SCARED

One of the most amazing things about listening to my Pastor Andy Stanley of Northpoint Church is that he answers questions I didn't know to ask. Recently his message was a crazy-pants intersection of the ancient book of wisdom I read daily and my life.

Whatever your belief system is (even if you don't subscribe to a belief system), this story's for you. He talked about the story of Jesus gathering with some fishermen. Back in that time, they fished all night, cleaned out the nets, dried them off, and then went to sleep because they had been up all night.

That morning when they were all done, Jesus said, "Go and fish again."

They were all like, "C'mon man, I'm tired. I'm exhausted."

But Jesus was all like, "Yeah, okay, but do it anyway."

Then Peter said, "Okay, because you said so, I will."

I mean, that in itself is super amazing. How quickly do we listen to the "whisper" inside us? I'd like to think it would be instant for me, in the way it was for Peter, but sometimes it takes me a hot minute.

Anyway, because they listened, their nets were filled up like nothing they had ever seen before. That trip made them so rich they didn't have to fish for a very long time.

But then they were called to become fishers of men. Oh boy. When we listen to that inner whisper and receive abundance and blessings, we are soon called to do more with those blessings and abundance.

I heard that whisper to scale my business and shift my life for a long time. I was scared, nervous, and afraid to let go of my 32 one-on-one clients so that I could serve more qualified clients. Yet in one year, I got 11,000 people I was able to serve. And after that I launched a program showing others how to do the same.

Whatever you believe, I know you are here on purpose, with purpose. What is your version of "Put the net on the other side?" I don't know your answer, but I hope your response to the whisper is, "Because you said so, I will," as you cast that net over.

## IT ISN'T BROKEN IF IT DOESN'T WORK IN THE FIRST TEN MINUTES

To thank my team for a hard-worked year, I took them to D.C. to the show of my good friend and coaching client, Justin Guarini. He was in Season One of *American Idol*. The "Little Sweet" character of Diet Dr. Pepper was starring in the Britney Spears music-filled delicious show, *Once Upon a One More Time*.

Before we left for the trip, I was on a call with Justin, harassing him about getting his slides done. Justin and I were partnering on a course, "How to Successfully Audition for a Broadway Show." Anyway, he shared his plan on the "when" to get it done after the holiday because, "I'll have more time once the show opens in a few weeks."

I was so confused because we were headed to the show that weekend. If the show hadn't opened yet, what were we going to see?

Forgive my Broadway ignorance, but what I didn't get was this: When a show is first being created, it is workshopped and changed after every performance. So, in addition to performing two shows a day, the actors have five hours of practice where they change and tweak things due to the previous audience's reaction.

Every. Single. Day. For months on end.

This is called "Workshopping."

In fact, it takes about seven years of changing and tweaking before a show officially makes it to Broadway.

Whoa.

Seven years of tweaking and testing before a hit? They go and do it every single day, knowing that's what they have to do in order to have the success they are looking for. But the payout is worth it because if the show does get to Broadway, the actors actually get equity in the show.

It's interesting that most of us expect incredibly successful results the first time we try something—without even putting in a lot of effort—or thinking we must be destined to fail.

That's kind of crazy, right?

After I picked up my slack jaw, I said, "So Justin, if you understand you, it take seven years for a show to make it. Are you willing to give your webinar a few tweaks to make sure it is successful?"

He realized the connection and said, "Wow. I never saw that before. Yes, I am willing to do all that I need to in order to make this a hit!"

How about you, dear reader? How about you start thinking about this a bit differently—not as a one-time show that must work, but instead that every action you take will provide more insight into what will work best. Everything. The good, the bad, the ugly. All on your way to the greatest Broadway Hit of all time—in your niche.

Your audience is waiting for you to do exactly that.

# IN CONCLUSION

## You Can, And You Will

**THEY DID IT.** I did it. We did it.

We set out on something others may see as small, but to us, it wasn't. It was a symbol of setting your sights on a goal and then working to accomplish it.

I volunteered as a coach for Girls on the Run, and one recent Saturday we ran our 5k race. It was 55 degrees out, with a slight mist in the air and the weather was perfect. Even better was the joy these kids had, and the pride they felt after working toward a goal and accomplishing it.

When we had our final meet-up on the following Monday, I asked them why they were thankful that they came. They all said that hadn't thought they could do it at the start of the semester, and then they did. They were happy, relieved, proud... you know, all the things.

They set out to accomplish something they didn't think they could do but took a step forward anyway. With each step, they got stronger. And faster. They believed more in themselves. That is what brought them the "I did it!" moment of crossing the finish line. Literally and figuratively.

The same emotions you have when you set your sights on any goal and move from, "I want it, but can I do it?" to "This may not work, but I am going to try anyway," to "This may actually be possible," to "Wow! I did it!"

It all starts with a desire and moving forward despite uncertainty. There is literally no way to be certain until you actually do it.

As we come to the end of this book journey together, my question for you is this: What's one goal you want to achieve that you aren't sure is possible, but that doesn't stop you from wanting it? Is there one thing you can do today to make it possible?

As you embark on your journey to becoming an anti-hustle-and-grind Powerful Professional, choosing to have a Lifestyle and Empire Business at the same time, the journey may look long. It may feel impossible. You aren't always going to be sure you can do it.

Then, you'll take a step anyway. And another. And another.

Each step brings you one step closer to crossing the finish line to your goals.

You may not believe yet that you can do it, so borrow some of my belief that you can. Take one step toward that goal today and soon you will be rounding the bend where the finish line appears.

And know that I'll be at the finish line with a big sign with leopard print letters, cheering the loudest in the crowd as you do.

You can, and you will.

# ⏻ THE POWERFUL PROFESSIONALS MOTTO

*Powerful Professionals* don't make excuses. **They make things happen**.

*Powerful Professionals* are in control of their business.

They are not victims. If something needs to change, they don't dream it would be different. **They make it different**.

*Powerful Professionals* know they were not created to fail.

They were created to **thrive**, and success is the **greatest response** to those who told them they can't. **They don't get even, they get ahead**.

Powerful Professionals choose to surround themselves with those who **inspire, encourage, and empower**.

*Powerful Professionals* recognize there is an **abundance** of business to be had. They choose who to work with, instead of others choosing to work with them, and they joyfully say "no" to cheap jerk-faces.

*Powerful Professionals* are not distracted by the latest shiny object. They are focused on proven strategies that fit in their sweet spot of gifts and talents.

*Powerful Professionals* know that their passions **are not an accident. They are their God-given superpowers**.

*Powerful Professionals* do not waste a dollar out of their pocket, minute of their time, or ounce of their talent. Yet, they can't invest fast enough in the tools they need to get them to where they want to go.

*Powerful Professionals* **do not compromise** on things most important to them. They are flexible in their "how" but never flexible in their "why." Family and faith are not a distraction **but a driving force.**

*Powerful Professionals* know that success doesn't always happen on the first try or second or even the third. But success is **inevitable** to those who keep trying. They don't give up when things get hard. **They push harder.**

*Powerful Professionals* don't wish for change. **They are the change.**

I am a *Powerful Professional*. Are you?

**#powertribe**

# ACKNOWLEDGMENTS

**THIS BOOK IS** dedicated first to God and His patience in getting me to listen. I'm a slow learner but finally, I've got it. I take time to listen now and actually act on what I hear. God is funny and just like He knows every feather on every bird's back, He knows me and my every thought and need, and greets me just the way I need... with humor, care, and love.

Right behind God, and almost as tall, is Ian, aka The Tall One. Since we met, you have told me I should write this book. You challenged me to tell these stories and share my insights, believing they would change the world. Just like the whispers from God, it took me a hot minute to listen and believe you, but for all of our late-night chats, funny text messages, knowing looks and champagne toasts on planes, I am forever grateful and love you to the moon and back.

Next up are my girls, Bella and Kate. You are my "why" and inspire me every day. I am so grateful I learned before it was too late that being present for your most important moments was more important than working "harder" and trying to achieve. If not for you, I may have never changed what I did day to day, and never could have eventually impacted thousands. As we talk about often, thank you for the impact you allow me to make every single day and the impact you make on the world as well.

To my parents, Jack and Gloria Walsh, I will always remember that day we came out of church, and you told me that your purpose was to support mine and that you wanted to move to Georgia so I could reach the world that was waiting to hear from me. You love my kids and each other like nothing I have ever seen, and if Ian and I can emulate you someday, I will be forever grateful.

To my ride-or-die, Kelly LeMay, for believing in this book topic and championing it all along the way and leading the journey with me at each stage—and for making sure this book got done on time. We kid that you have to be an octopus to get all that you do done at the same time, but really, what is your secret? And can we bottle it and sell it?

To Team Power: Ashley MacDonell, Diane Laffoon, Jack Hollingsworth, Kelly Moderwell, Tanya Vestuto, Laurie Rollings, and Kate Gilchrist... you are the peanut butter to my jelly and without you, we are soggy bread that leaves a bad aftertaste; with you, the perfect combination of sweet and crunchy. You are important, you matter, and I am so grateful you use your gifts to bless our people and the world.

Now, this next list is going to get me in trouble for leaving someone out, but I don't have the restraint to skip it. It's the fuel to my fire, the friend to my ship, the joy to my day, my posse of the most incredible individuals who cheered on this project and my everyday:

Brittney Walton, Leslie Streeter, Sabrina and Tristan Truscott, Justin Guarini, and Scott Whitaker: Let's keep the bodies buried and have a dance party instead, mm'kay?

Thankful also for my Jersey crew: Lauren Fisher, Karen Tucker, Amy Lober, Lindsey Larkin, Larisa Weaver (where's your book... I want to read it!), and all of your families. My Georgia crew: Sarah Jones, Bridgit Motes, Erin Watt, Tammy Dugger, Jacque House, Megan Melchiors, and all of your families, Ariana Chedgy, Yvonne Johnson, Hilee Moua, and all of the other king's horsemen and women who put this queen back together again.

To Demi Stevens for your editing magic, always. You are the unsung hero of thousands. I am so glad I get to call you mine.

And to Jennifer Dorsey and Vanessa Campos for believing enough in me to launch your publishing house with my book. I love you two and can't wait to celebrate our vision with a best-selling book.

And to you, dear reader, for wanting more and for doing something about it. You are about to discover what it means to be a Powerful Professional, and I can't wait to see how you impact the world. You are exactly what we all need right now.

Thank you for reading.